SPIRITUAL

Delivery

The Birthing of a Life of Freedom

Dell Mavia Johnson Walters BSN, RN

SPIRITUAL DELIVERY

The Birthing of a Life of Freedom

Dell Mavia Johnson Walters, BSN, RN

Published By

Eagles Word Christian Publisher, LLC
New York

DEDICATION

I dedicate this book to a very important and powerful group of individuals who are responsible for guiding others through difficult situations. This group of people are referred to as mentors, and can range from those who provide encouragement and hope to others, to those who devote a portion of themselves to interceding with them in prayer until the final victory. An intercessor is one who stands between the person needing help and the enemy, and many times, those intercessors/midwives empathize with their own actual experiences.

Mentors or intercessors, whom I shall call spiritual midwives, assist new disciples as they struggle to navigate from a season of bondage to a new life of freedom in Christ.

TABLE OF CONTENTS

FOREWORD

When Nicodemus came to Jesus with questions, during the conversation Jesus said to him, 'You must be born again.' This statement has been preached by Christian ministers throughout the ages, and is indeed fundamental to the Christian doctrine.

In this book we explore what it truly means to be 'born again.' This book looks at the phenomenon of natural birth, and synchronizes that process with the process of spiritual birth.

Ms. Walters uses examples from her personal experiences working as a registered nurse and her training as a midwife, to show how being born again correlates with spiritual delivery from sin, oppression or spiritual attacks. Additionally, she utilizes the story of Job to bring out Biblical truths and their applications.

Each chapter is dedicated to one of the elements of childbirth, relating that element to spiritual delivery.

This is truly a revelation of the divine mind of Christ and God, and represents a true work of art.

Evangelist Judy Howard

PREFACE

As a registered nurse I was educated in the care of the body and the prevention of illnesses. As an addendum to my preliminary training, I was given the opportunity to study and train as a midwife in Jamaica, and this latter training completely changed my life. This training placed me in the position of simultaneously being a mentor to a new mother, as well as assisting in bringing new life into the world.

Midwives follow in the steps of great men and women of God in the Bible. People such as:

- Elijah who mentored Elisha
- Elizabeth who mentored Mary
- Mordecai who mentored Esther
- Naomi who mentored Ruth
- Moses who mentored Joshua; and
- Paul, who mentored Timothy

On a personal level, I am grateful for the mentorship of Elise Thomas who mentored me for years. In midwife school, God led me to assemble my class of student midwives for a weekly prayer meeting and my mentor, Elise Thomas, confidently joined us in our first session. She believed in me, and helped me to find and walk in my purpose. She believed in me as an author even before I was able to write my first book.

Ultimately, God commissioned me as a midwife in the Kingdom of God. Consequently, my purpose is to help to guide new disciples through the delivery process of the new birth; assisting in delivering healthy mothers and babies. God has equipped me with the necessary knowledge which helps me to understand the delivery of souls in the spiritual realm.

If God has called you to deliver souls into the Kingdom, do not hesitate, because if there is a delay in delivering a baby, it can result in complications and even death. It is expedient that new disciples, therefore, be delivered in a timely manner; if not, there is the possibility of regression.

You are called to be a midwife like Naomi—skillfully helping to deliver souls, like Ruth, who are lost.

INTRODUCTION

Psalm 22:8 *"He trusted on the Lord that he would deliver him: let him deliver him, seeing he delighted in him. 9) But thou art he that took me out of the womb: thou didst make me hope when I was upon my mother's breast. 10) I was cast upon thee from the womb: thou art my God from my mother's belly."*

Everywhere we look there is evidence of life. From the birds flying around chirping happily, the flowers with their sweet fragrance in the wind, and animals grazing on green grass in pastures under the sunlight.

There is also evidence of death. We see it in the trees and shrubs whose branches are dried up; and in dry areas where there were once pools of water. Thankfully, there is a season and cycle for new life. With the rain comes new life, new growth and new springs of water.

God has given us the choice of life or death. I choose life, and this is why I wrote this book, and I hope you choose life too.

New life comes about when the fetus is nourished and moves from an intra-uterine position of restriction to an extra-uterine life of freedom. It is a mammoth task for the midwife—who skillfully and safely guides delivery of the unborn child through the birth canal. Midwives are invaluable—not only do they provide assistance for the baby, they provide a strong resource for the mother—reassuring her with each push. It is an unselfish act of love.

Likewise, mentors called by God, are valuable in the Kingdom of God because they help in the process of delivering precious souls for Jesus. As stated previously, Naomi was the mentor (midwife) who helped deliver Ruth. Mordecai mentored and helped deliver Esther. Paul helped deliver Timothy; Moses mentored Joshua.

You, too, might have been mentored by someone; and now it is your time to be a midwife to someone else. Many people are struggling in the womb (after coming to Christ) and need help and attention to successfully navigate these difficult times. As stated before, timing is important because delivery is time sensitive, and we do not want to lose a soul. *"It is not His will that any should perish but that all sinners should come to repentance."*

As we embark on this journey of spiritual delivery, I make the following declarations. I declare—

- Life over conception of new life
- Life over the grounding of the egg to the wall of the uterus
- Life over the placenta adequately nourishing the fetus.
- Life and power to overcome the obstacles at birth.
- Life over delivery of newborns
- Life as newborns take the first breath and transitions to extra-uterine existence.
- Life over the breastmilk that nurtures the newborns.
- Life over newborn growth and development
- Life over purpose in newborns

If you are reading this book and you are experiencing any kind of struggle, I am here to encourage you that God will complete what He has started. He will deliver you. Your time has come. It is your birthing season. This is your ninth month. It is your season of expectancy and anticipation. God will lift the weight from you that you have been carrying for so long. Be ready with the right attitude to push through the pain.

Being confident of this very thing, that He which hath begun a good work in you will perform it until the day of Jesus Christ. Philippians 1:6.

Chapter One

Purpose is Within You

In the Book of Job, we read that Job was tested and tried. In his torment he looked back to his beginnings—the womb.

He said in Job 1:21

> *Naked came I from my mother's womb and naked shall I return."*

That's where it starts for all of us. Even though Job condemned the fruit of the womb for having brought forth life and light (Job 3:10&11), the fact that he came from a fertile womb predicted the outcome of his spiritual conflict. Job's suffering not only caused him to regret his birth, but he even cursed his conception; such was the pain of his suffering. However, without conception, there is no fulfillment.

Conception. What is it? The dictionary defines it as follows:

> **Conception** — the action of conceiving a child or offspring. It is bringing into being or bringing into existence.

Conception can also mean an idea or beginning. The Bible says in Genesis 1:26:

> *Let us make man in our image after our likeness…*

Before God actually created man, He conceived the idea, so from conception, man was given purpose. ***Purpose is within you***. After God conceived man, He created him and gave him life. The life of a person spans from its creation as a fetus to its cessation—from conception to death. With life comes the ability to move, feed, reproduce and respond.

Life is defined as:

> *the condition that distinguishes animals and plants from inorganic matter, including the capacity for growth, reproduction, functional activity and continual change preceding death.*

According to Genesis 2:7

> *The Lord God formed man out of the dust of the ground and breathed into his nostrils the breath of life; and man became a living soul.*

No one can explain how the heart of a fetus miraculously starts beating at three weeks in-utero. It is one of the mysteries of life.

Utero/Early Development

Let us take a brief look at the development of the baby in utero. During early development in the uterus, the protective sac and placenta sustains, nourishes and protects the fetus. The fetus continues to grow in the mother's womb until it reaches term.

This natural birth helps us to understand the miracle of the spiritual birth. At the moment of the new birth, a person is immediately given a new spirit and new life begins. After the new life begins, there is a process of

2

development leading to delivery of the mind to agree with the mind of Christ. That takes time.

As Christians, we also begin intra uterine, and much like a natural birth, it requires much pushing and pressing. There will be discomfort, there will be distress, you will have the pain of contractions. Do not give up. Stay the course. God will see you through.

God Shows Us Purpose

I had a dream in May, 2018 in which I was standing in the path of dirty, raging water. Suddenly two strong arms grabbed my hands and lifted me to the safety of the second story of the two-floor building before me. As I was pulled to safety I was terrified of the raging water, so I continued watching it instead of the strong arms that rescued me. After being pulled to safety, I recognized that I had a small baby bump, and that puzzled me. God gave me a word in the dream from Isaiah 41:10 *"Fear thou not for I am with thee, be not dismayed for I am thy God. I will strengthen thee, yea, I will help thee, I will uphold thee with the right hand of my righteousness."*

God also reassured me with Isaiah 43:2 *"When thou passest through the waters, I will be with thee, and through the rivers, they shall not overflow thee: when thou walkest through the fire thou shalt not be burned, neither shall the flame kindle upon thee.*

Two weeks later, on June 2, 2018, I had severe lower right abdominal pain. I was worried that I was suffering from the pain of appendicitis and might need an appendectomy. That night while trying to sleep despite the pain, I dreamt that the hand came again to rescue me. The hand pinched and pulled my abdomen at the same

3

spot where the pain was. It was very painful; however, the hand miraculously pulled a lump through the skin without an incision. The pain stopped immediately, and my body was healed. The hand then presented me with a bundle swaddled in a white glowing mantle with a shimmering silver lining. As the mantle fell open, I saw the glorious form of a baby's head shining with what looks like the glory of God. I could not stare at it as it was too glorious.

Many times God will show us things to come through dreams, because things are accomplished in the spirit realm before they are manifested in the natural realm. I believe that the dream illustrated what would happen in my life in the future. That night, I delivered the promise of God in the spiritual realm.

> Isaiah 59:2—*"My Spirit that is upon thee, and my words which I have put in thy mouth, shall not depart out of thy mouth, nor out of the mouth of thy seed, nor out of the mouth of thy seed's seed, saith the Lord, from henceforth and forever."* To God be the glory.

I am able to give praise to God because He showed me that whatever I would face, I would be victorious. I am coming out! My shackles are broken, I am set free! I am delivered!

We read in Matthew 11:28:

> *Come unto me all ye that labour and are heavy laden and I will give you rest.*

The Body of Christ experiences several difficulties, complication and obstructions; however, the Lord Jesus will deliver us safely. We will not die in childbirth.

We get broken by hard times in life and in these difficult seasons we need to be rescued and delivered. A **labor** of love nurtures the gift or promise that God gave us like the welcoming rain coming to renew life.

The Bible puts it this way in 1 Corinthians 15:58 – "*Be ye stedfast, unmoveable, always abounding in the work of the Lord forasmuch as ye know that your labor is not in vain in the Lord.*"

The Mechanism of Labor

Just as it is important in the natural to know the mechanism of labor, it is equally important in the spiritual realm.

1. *The Lie*. In the natural, the positioning is known as the *Lie*. Positioning in the spiritual is just as important as in the natural, because you need to be looking upward toward heaven in expectancy.
2. *Attitude*. It is necessary to be in a state of expectancy and readiness, with your mind bent towards pushing through the pain.
3. *Presentation*. This is basically your determination to go all the way. It goes hand in hand with your attitude.
4. *Position*. It is necessary to identify where you are in regards to your thinking, as labor progresses.
5. *The Station* is the measurement of the progress.
6. *Strength* is the ingredient needed for endurance.

The mechanism of labor is incorporated into the seven cardinal movements of labor, and we will explore these in the next chapter.

Chapter Two

The Seven Cardinal Movements
of Labor

The Seven Cardinal Movements of Labor, while painful, are nonetheless stunning and it is a privilege to assist in this process as a midwife.

The process begins as follows:

Engagement—a state of anticipation and expectancy; a state of preparation and readiness for delivery. It is when a person's focus is locked in.

Descent is the downward plunge of the baby as it navigates through the birth canal towards the light.

Flexion is the molding of the head. Attitude is bended under the pressure of pushing your way through, and this pressure is accompanied by the pain of pressing.

Internal Rotation is the turning of the fetus' head. Internal rotation occurs as a result of resistance as the head moves through the birth canal.

Extension is where the force of the contraction pain presses the head downward and there is crowning. The head is delivered but the body is not yet released or free.

Restitution is the external turning or rotation of the head to realign with the body.

Expulsion is final stage of delivery and this marks the complete expulsion of the entire body. The baby takes its first breath of life at this stage.

Following expulsion is the cutting of the umbilical cord and delivery of the placenta. At this state the baby moves from dependence to independence; from darkness into light; from confinement to freedom.

Application to the Spiritual Realm

This description gives us a clear understanding of how spiritual birth is accomplished. The same terms used to describe the natural process is also applicable in the spiritual process. For further clarification we will look at these and other terminology as defined by the dictionary.

Engagement according to Wikipedia, is arrangement to do something or go somewhere in a fixed time. It is when a person is lined up and locked in. You must have a made-up mind to come through to victory.

Quickening. It is necessary to have lightening (or movement), because if a baby stays in one place too long (in other words failure to progress) it will complicate the delivery process.

Breaking. There must be a breaking of the waters for the labor to progress. Therefore, in the spiritual realm, we must be broken to receive the blessing God has for us.

Stretching and thinning is necessary for movement and growth. Stretching is brought on through struggles.

Contraction is the pain encountered while we are being stretched.

Descent. Just as there must be downward movement for the fetus to get to the light, when a person experiences an emotional down, the Lord lifts them up.

Rotation. During the process, there is an internal rotation of the head before it is delivered. When this occurs in a Christian's life, it marks the change which occurs in the mind of the Believer. Our mind must line up with the mind of Christ. It is the beginning of complete delivery.

Molding. In a normal situation, the head of the baby leads the way into the birth canal for delivery. The pressure in the canal molds the head into position. The parietal skull bone overlaps, reducing head size to accommodate an easy delivery. God molds and forms the Christian into His will for his or her life.

Crowning occurs when the head is partially delivered and is visible from temple to temple. This resembles the crown or reward you will receive for the journey from which you have come.

Restitution. After the head is delivered, there is a complete turning to align head with the body for its delivery.

Expulsion is the complete delivery of the person from mental and emotional bondage, bringing joy and rest to their life.

Following expulsion the umbilical cord is cut. Spiritually speaking when God has delivered us from bondage, we must *cut connection* to our past life and darkness.

As you navigate your spiritual birth canal, remember that you are coming out. The labor process is painful, but it brings new life, new love and new joy.

The Lord will give you strength to endure.

"Many are the afflictions of the righteous; but the Lord delivereth him out of them all"

"Bless the Lord O my soul, and forget not all his benefits. Who forgiveth all thine iniquities; who healeth all thy diseases."

A Natural and Spiritual Connection

As an intercessor, we often experience the same feelings the other person is experiencing. I believe this is similar to what Jesus experienced for us. Scripture says He was touched with the feelings of our infirmities.

"For we have not an high priest which cannot be touched with the feeling of our infirmities; but was in all points tempted like as we are, yet without sin".
Hebrews 4:15.

My Personal Experience.

In April 2020, one of my family members went for a routine endoscopy to check his pancreas. This happened at the time when all procedures were cancelled due to the developing covid 19 pandemic. During the procedure, the clinician made an unscheduled incision and no bowel preparation was done before sedation.

As a result, he woke up in excruciating pain, developed pancreatitis and had to be treated at the hospital. His pain became more severe, and he was later diagnosed with paralytic ileus. Along with the pain intervention, multiple tests were done, but he still got no relief. Daily his condition deteriorated until unfortunately he was diagnosed with covid 19. He was admitted to ICU, intubated and placed on a ventilator. His complete

10

diagnoses were paralytic ileus, pancreatitis and Covid 19.

My family was in turmoil as his condition became worse each day. We cried out to God—binding the illness and petitioning God for healing. God's Word says, *"whatsoever ye shall bind on earth shall be bound in heaven and whatsoever ye shall loose on earth shall be loosed in heaven" Matthew 18:18.*

Before he had been admitted to ICU, he had multiple diagnostic tests because of the pain he was experiencing. He was not able to speak with me due to the severity of the pain. When he was able, he called to say he was back from the ICU; however they would be taking him back for more tests. We prayed asking God to intervene.

The following day his pain resolved, he was out of ICU, eating and passing stool for the first time. He also requested to be transferred to a research hospital nearby because the doctors were unable to diagnose and treat him despite the tests.

Prior to these events, I had a dream that someone dressed in a white long-sleeve shirt and black pants visited my home and walked to the edge of the lake behind my house. He made two steps in the water and suddenly sank in the canal with water up to his neck. I saw the danger but was unable to get close enough to assist. I stretched out a line to him for him to hold, however his eyes were on me but his hands appeared trapped, and he was stuck.

The Lord Jesus showed me that the interpretation of the dream was that someone would be in a difficult situation and would need to be rescued. That line that I had sent out in the dream is a "Prayer Line" which was the strategy needed to rescue this man from drowning.

When my family member arrived at the new hospital, his tests were positive for the covid 19 virus. Immediately he started having labored breathing. The difficult decision was made to have him intubated and placed on a ventilator.

Prayer was lifted to God for him from all over the world—wherever I could find someone who was willing to come into agreement for his healing and deliverance. We were to wrestle and fight a brutal bloody battle on our knees for his life.

I was at the forefront of the battle petitioning and interceding with God. I would receive updates from the doctor and inform the prayer team of the details. It was a tough battle. Days on the ventilator became weeks, weeks became months (or felt like months). We cried out to God, remained instant and focused in prayer, refusing to give up. God kept him stable. The Lord is faithful. Members of the family joined in and prayed to God daily, and we all prayed together on Sundays and Wednesdays.

On the fourth day of his ventilation, I felt a tightening around my temple like a headband. My blood pressure was elevated and I became tired, anxious and afraid. I was about to learn the greatest lesson of faith and patience (or my lack thereof).

After praying for weeks—(or months), God remained silent. When the Lord is silent it is a cold and depressing place. I lost my health, my ability to sleep, and my strength while waiting on God.

The Lord had given me a Word before this event from

> *Isaiah 43:2 "when thou passest through the waters, I will be with thee; and through the rivers, they shall not overflow thee; when thou walkest through the fire, thou shalt not be burned; neither shall the flame kindle upon thee."*

I was reminded by God of this Word. In the days to come I walked in red hot fire. I only survived because of this Word. I walked in dangerously raging waters, but this Word helped me to keep my head above the waters—but just barely.

As I fasted and interceded for my family member, my health began to fail due to lack of sleep and rest. I was not sleeping because I was fearful and anxious that my family member was going to die. Waiting and watching him on the ventilator and the uncertainty was too much for me to bear. I was now crying to God to help me as I was thrown into deep depression and asked God, "why are you taking so long?"

The Lord showed me that I should listen to the hundreds of scriptures in my daily devotional, "*The Word for Today*" that I send out daily to listeners. I listened but I needed more. I called out to others for help to pray for me as I was having difficulty falling asleep. I took muscle relaxant which did not work well. I was still anxious.

I was reluctant to go to the hospital or an urgent care facility, as the pandemic was raging. I realized I had to face fear. I had underestimated fear and found out I was not equipped. I called a registered nurse colleague who accompanied me to the urgent care.

My blood pressure was very high. I was informed that I should go home, take Benadryl and get rest. I tried the Benadryl for two nights; however, that did not work. I was still anxious. I would sometimes fall asleep and wake up after two hours, believing it was morning. I tried relaxing by drinking chamomile tea, cinnamon tea, ginger and garlic tea. Inspite of this, I would only fall asleep at 1:00 AM—feeling every attack of anxiety.

My thoughts raced all night and refused to slow down. My blood pressure was high, and my pulse was bounding and loud. It was so loud it prevented me from falling asleep. I felt pain in my back, my hands, my feet and all over my body. My head felt heavy. I had a tingling sensation in my hands and could not find a comfortable position to place them. Most of all I wrestled with suicidal ideation. My greatest fear was telling my family because I did not want to scare them or cause them to worry. So, I hid all the knives in the house.

I cried out to God! Lord, heal me! If you do not come to my rescue I will die. Where should I go but to You? I am completely surrendered waiting for You to heal me. I cried Lord Jesus if you speak to my mind, it will slow down. If you Lord Jesus speak to my heart rate it will calm down. If you speak to my blood pressure it will become normal in Jesus' name. I waited patiently on God, then I fell into a deep, restful sleep. Glory to God!

I had to pray for hours each day to fall asleep each night as I was battling depression and anxiety. My days were sometimes up, but most times down. The Lord was teaching me the ninefold fruits of the Spirit.

I learned patience when the lab misplaced my urine study results that had been done for my new job, and called for me to repeat the urine test. The Lord taught me to remain calm and carry all lies and miseries to Him. I remained calm as the Lord Jesus has my back and the enemy is no match for my God. The Lord taught me to trust Him while I wait on my family member's healing.

As I struggled to fall asleep at nights, it might be late; however, God always showed up to give me rest. God is faithful, He always shows up. Sometimes we do not recognize His presence, but He is there. I speak to the negative thoughts in my mind to be subject to the Word of God; then I give God thanks. I thank God for today, for all who were blessed to see today, for the promises He fulfilled and the blessings I received from Him today. I thank God that He has me, my health and my weaknesses in the palm of His hand. I thank Him that His grace is sufficient to keep me. I am so thankful that He preserved my mind, body and spirit. I turn my worry into worship.

God continues to teach me to trust Him. When my nurse colleague was late picking me up, God asked me, 'how do you know she is coming?' I responded that she gave me her word and we have a good relationship. God then asked me "why don't you trust *Me*, I gave you my Word, I always show up, and we have a great relationship." I asked God to forgive me. I need You Jesus, help my unbelief.

The Lord God taught me to live one day at a time, trusting Him. I was going through an emotional turmoil watching my family member's health deteriorate. On the other hand, God wanted me to trust Him as He reminded me, "It is only a test."

Thank you, Lord, that I am learning to trust you and learning how to remain calm. I thank You Lord because You always show up; we have a good relationship; and You gave me your Word. When it pleases you, you will move.

I wrote in my journal: I worship God in the most difficult times. Thou art worthy oh Lord, to receive glory, honor and praise. You created us for your pleasure, so we glorify You. Thou art the God who worketh wonders, thou hast made known thy strength among the people.

I wake up thankful despite the stormy nights, every day is a blessing. I am grateful for the goodness of God.

My family member is still asleep on the ventilator. His condition is morbid and might get worse. Every day we expect it to be his last. Still God's plan is always best. Sometimes the process is painful and difficult. I must not forget that when God is silent, He is doing something great for us.

The Lord has refreshed me. I now have a renewed desire to read God's Word at length.

I read all 14 chapters of Zechariah but spent time meditating on Zech 4:7

> *"Who art thou O great mountain? Before Zerubbabel thou shalt become a plain: and he shall bring forth the headstone thereof with shoutings, crying, "Grace, grace unto it."*

The Lord delivered my soul. He blessed me and healed me with His Word. My mind was alert and responsive. The Holy Spirit gave me good understanding of God's Word.

I walk in God consciousness through the Holy Spirit of Jesus Christ who renewed my spirit. I enquired of God why I was still having difficulty sleeping. God wanted me to be awake to show me revelations. His Word! His Word!

His Word is a covenant. I asked Holy Spirit to reveal to me what God wanted to teach me. He led me to Zechariah 4:6

> *"...then He answered and spake unto me, saying, this is the word of the Lord unto Zerubbabel, saying, Not by might, nor by power, but by my Spirit, saith the Lord of hosts".* He said this mountain before you shall be a plain.

He taught me the vision of Zechariah. So now when I read His Word in the presence of the Holy Spirit, He will give me His peace. Isaiah 26:3 *"Thou wilt keep him in perfect peace whose mind is stayed on thee, because he trusteth in thee."*

Wisdom From Above

The strategy God gave me is to keep my mind focused on Him. Keep meditating on Him and trusting Him, then I shall lay down to sleep, and my sleep shall be sweet and peaceful. He will then cause me to have visions and revelations and victory in Jesus Christ.

I realized where God was taking me. I had an active morning prayer routine but would fall asleep at nights most times without praying. Now I get quality sleep only when I pray, meditate and listen to the Word of God. Thank you, Jesus, because you live, I shall live, my family member also shall live. I shall not die but live and declare the works of the Lord. Amen. The Lord showed me that "I am with you to deliver you" saith the Lord.

It is in Him we live and move and have our being. So, we overcome by the blood of the Lamb and by the word of our testimony. I will bless the Lord at all times, His praise shall continually be in my mouth.

As I waited on God for my family member's healing it felt like we were being defeated. The Lord showed me to look away from the situation. Look to Jesus and focus on each day's assignments. He taught me to remove my own expectations and live one day at a time. The battle is already won. Give thanks for every day of life. Even if I am sick, I should give thanks because I have hope. When I get out of bed, I must pray for someone who needs healing. God will show up and heal me too.

> *My grace is sufficient to keep you. Finally, my brethren be strong in the Lord and in the power of his might.*

God showed me that I am coming out by speaking to my mind that I am being delivered.

This mental situation resembles the overwhelming pressure of the molding of the head in a natural birth. The molding of the head feels like crushing, but the head is almost out.

God continued to endow me with His wisdom. I learnt these lessons. This too shall pass! I am coming out and

God has set me in a large place. The battle is already won. I must keep my eyes on Jesus, pay attention to my assignment and minister to someone who needs Jesus. Wake up and live one day at a time! Renounce sickness. Live! Live! Live!

I also learnt how to use my authority. Each day as I wake up: I take **authority** over my day. As it is written in Matthew 18:18–20 *"whatsoever ye shall bind on earth shall be bound in heaven: whatsoever ye shall loose on earth shall be loosed in heaven."* So, I bind the strongholds and plans of the enemy. I speak to fear, doubt, unbelief, sicknesses and lies with the truth of the Word of God.

The Word says that we are cast down but not destroyed. I confess my God and Savior Jesus Christ, His Kingship and His Lordship. I exercise faith, by hearing and repeating the Word of God. I play videos and listen to scriptures. I also write scriptures and hang them on my walls at home.

Everyday my family member remains alive we are thankful and faithfully wait on God for his healing.

I live in victory, revisiting past situations that I overcame. I learned to live one day at a time as tomorrow is promised to no man. I worship God because He is alive. I am healed by His stripes. God delivers my mind as I thank Him. He is on time. He gave me His word. I am learning the qualities of God as I have a more intimate relationship with Him.

God delivered me from suicidal thoughts; I faced them and told them they are no match for my God. Sometimes when I see the kitchen knife these thoughts appear. I slay them with the Word of God. The Lord is my keeper. The Lord God delivered me from sleepless nights, Hallelujah! Thank you, Jesus. He delivered me from being frightened and from irritability at every sound. I am delivered and so I praise God's name. I am forever thankful; I am eternally grateful because I am abundantly blessed. I told my problems that they are no match for my God.

As David encouraged himself in the Lord, so too we must speak the Word to encourage ourselves. David also sang the praises of God

I remind myself, "Trust in the Lord with all of my heart and lean not to my own understanding." "Thy word have I hid in my heart that I will not sin against thee."

It is only a test. Hold on! I sing to the Lord "Lord I believe, Lord I believe, all things are possible. Lord, I believe." Glory to God. "After you've done all, you can, just stand." Stand! The battle belongs to the Lord.

Sicknesses, covid-19, pain, depression and anxiety are no match for my God. I walk in faith as my family member was still in the ICU on the ventilator. I realized it is a process and I must fight my way through.

What I am relating to you are some of the labor pains I experienced while waiting for the deliverance of my family member.

I manifested the signs of depression. Everything felt different. I was awakened by every sound or noise; I became a very light sleeper. I felt afraid in the dark and afraid to fall asleep. I felt claustrophobic and always wanted to be outside. My mind was overactive. There was pounding, bounding and loud pulses; pain to internal organs and extremities.

Each day I faced the fear that my family member would not recover. I faced the fear that the pandemic would rapidly increase the death rate. I also faced the fear of worsening depression and anxiety symptoms and suicidal thoughts.

If you find yourself experiencing these kinds of symptoms do not delay. Reach out to the suicide hotline for help.

Praise is the Key

The key to victory is telling God how great He is and speaking of all the wonderful things He has done. I continue to speak to my thoughts and remind them about the Word of God. I continued to record and repeatedly listen to videos of my devotional *"The Word for Today"* that I send out to WhatsApp listeners daily.

God said in His word "My strength is made perfect in weakness." So, I am learning to cast my cares on Him because He cares.

My Molding

During this molding time, there were several instructions I received from God that related to my personal life:

- Put Him first
- Eat healthy and drink enough water
- Exercise
- Get sunlight
- Live in faith, strength and the confidence of God

- Have fellowship with family and friends
- Rest

I also learned that while the pandemic continued, I could take herbs and teas which promote health; herbs such as turmeric, ginger, garlic, cinnamon, lemon, apple cider vinegar and onion.

Each day God also gave me a new scripture:

Proverbs 3:24 —When thou liest down, thou shalt not be afraid: yea, thou shalt lie down, and thy sleep shall be sweet.

Proverbs 3:33 — He blesseth the habitation of the just.

His secret is with the righteous. He giveth grace unto the lowly.

As I struggled through that season of **molding** I wondered when God would show up and heal me completely. He assured me that I should go to my desk and work, because He is with me, and He will sustain me. He reminded me that this is a test. Each day as I worked, I excelled in my job even though physically I felt like a mess. The Lord asked me to write each day's challenges and victories, as this is a test.

Stretching

As I said earlier, stretching occurs as a result of movement and growth. I was afraid to fall asleep. I dreaded the night because of the pain and difficulty to sleep. I was jumpy and easily frightened. I laid alert and could hear every sound. I could hear the pounding of my pulses in my temples. I was afraid to check my blood pressure. I was afraid and became anxious about any and everything. I needed immediate help!

This caused me to do some research on my health condition. I found that in addition to reading my bible, praying and worshiping God daily, these things helped:

Taking deep breaths every hour and releasing slowly.
Getting fresh air
Learning calming and relaxation techniques, I like a massage
Finding ways to laugh, (I like to watch comedies)
Exercising, stretching and walking outdoors
Most of all, being grateful.

Gratitude is the greatest therapy, because it keeps our mind on God. It allows us to see God as our Father, our Savior, our deliverer. We experience His love, life, light, liberty, laughter, labor of love and His listening ears.

I thank God He is the Bread of Life and I thank Him for His blood and His breath. I bless the Lord for He watches over me; He waters my soul and He walks with me.

Worship

Along with praise, there is worship. Worshipping God with songs of Zion takes us directly into the Throne Room. Some of the songs I sang were:

- o Because He lives, I can face tomorrow
- o I am no longer a slave to fear, I am a child of God
- o Amazing grace, how sweet the sound….my fears are gone, I've been set free
- o I will sing of the goodness of God

- My fear doesn't stand a chance when I am standing in your love
- His eye is on the sparrow and I know he watches over me.
- By the blood of Jesus, I prevailed over sickness
- He leads me beside still waters…he took me aside to be tested and tried

God seems to respond when we worship Him. He took me to Isaiah 45:2-3

> *"I will go before thee and make the crooked places straight; I will break in pieces the gates of brass and cut in sunder the bars of iron.*
>
> *And I will give thee the treasures of darkness, and hidden riches of secret places, that thou mayest know that I, the Lord, which call thee by name, am the God of Israel."*

As I continued to praise God, I still struggled because sometimes I felt like He was not there, but He continued to reassure me that this is a test, and He is a mountain-moving God.

I had breakfast with my God in the mornings and He fed me with His manna:

> *Isaiah 41:10 "Fear thou not; for I am with thee; Be not dismayed for I am thy God; I will strengthen thee, yea I will help thee, yea I will uphold thee with the right hand of my righteousness.*

To quell anxiety, He says,

> *Matthew 6:25 "Therefore I tell you do not be anxious about your life, what you will eat or what*

you will drink, nor about your body what you will put on. Is not life more than food, and the body more than clothing. (ESV)

Matthew 6:33-34 "But seek first the kingdom of God and His righteousness and all these things will be added to you" ESV

"Therefore, do not be anxious about tomorrow for tomorrow will be anxious for itself. Sufficient for the day is its own trouble." ESV

Philippians 4:6–8 –Be anxious for nothing, but in everything by prayer and supplication with thanksgiving let your requests be made known to God. NKJV

And the Peace of God which surpasses all understanding will guard your hearts and minds through Christ Jesus.

Finally, brethren, whatsoever things are true, whatsoever things are noble, whatsoever things are just, whatsoever things are pure, whatsoever things are lovely, whatsoever things are of good report; if there is any virtue, and if there is anything praiseworthy, meditate on these things."

I praise Him with spiritual songs:-

- ❖ Jesus, Jesus, precious Jesus, oh for grace to trust Him more
- ❖ His name is wonderful, Jesus my Lord
- ❖ Hallelujah, thine the glory, revive us again
- ❖ Thine is the kingdom, forever and ever and ever, Amen, amen, amen.

- ❖ Oh, how He loves me, I know not why I only cry, oh, how He loves me.
- ❖ Be not dismayed whatever betide, God will take care of you.
- ❖ He'll do it again, just take a look at where you are now and where you have been

Created for Praise

The Bible says that we were created to praise the Lord (Psalm 102:18), and this time of praise and worship convinced me that God wanted more of me. He wanted more of my attention –not just when my family member is dying or when I am struggling with anxiety. He wanted my complete attention. From then on, before going to bed I added an evening session of praise. Also, my morning routine consists of praying, reading the Word and worshipping God.

I visited a church with a friend and her husband who were pastors of the church. The pastor interceded for me, standing against my fears and negative emotions in the name of Jesus. He took authority in the spirit, breaking yokes and tearing down strongholds under the power of the Holy Spirit, and praying in the spirit for my strength during this season of *Stretching*.

He battled for the release of my mind, that I would walk with the mind Christ. He was my "midwife," patiently guiding me through the "birth canal" until I was delivered, physically, mentally and spiritually. I felt free! Glory to God! Thank you, Jesus.

I released the health and life of my family member into God's hands. It was not my weight to carry; he belongs to Jesus. I became free of anxiety, weariness and depression.

I worshipped God because He healed me, He delivered me and set me free. When I grew weary, the Lord would remind me to listen to the Word in the *Word for Today* devotional. Faith comes by hearing the Word of God. I cast all my burdens on Him because He cares.

God reminded me that I am the apple of His eyes; I am precious in His sight; I am chosen by God; I am made a little lower than the angels and crowned with glory and honor; I am engraved in the palm of God's hand; I am special to God; I am loved by God. I will praise You every day Lord Jesus!

Chapter Three

God's Word is Challenged

As happened in the cases of Eve and Jesus, the enemy comes to challenge the Word of God and the victories we've won. In a similar manner, the enemy returned to my bedroom, even after my initial deliverance.

One night my fight to sleep was so bad, that I thought I was about to die. I drew myself under God's arm and said "into thine hands I commit my spirit." My heart raced out of control—I had severe pain in my head, my chest, my back, my hands and my feet. I prayed, and I began to feel the presence of Jesus in the room. I eventually fell asleep. When I woke up the following morning, I was so grateful for another day. I give God glory for everything. I prayed even for those who hated me, begging God to have mercy on them and help them not to face these difficulties. I realized God is bigger than all problems and sicknesses.

God is always near. He always shows up. He does not give us more than we can bear. God comes with the truth that whatever we are going through is a lie from hell. God is all we need. God loves us, God loves me. He always makes a way. God gives us victory—we overcome by the blood of the Lamb and the word of our testimony. God is in control, thank you Jesus!

The following night I did not sleep at all. I went into periods of light sleep but not rest. I took two melatonin tablets, but they did not work well enough to make me sleep. I cried out to God for help again. I received a call from a pastor who often prayed with me on the phone. He prayed with me as I laid down to sleep; however, I got little rest. My thoughts turned to Job, who said "though He slay me still will I trust Him."

I woke up the next day with about two hours' rest. The Lord showed me that whatever rest He gave me was enough. He can keep me and sustain me with or without sleep. I thanked Him for a new day. I called the TBN prayer line and was prayed for. I was strengthened. I thanked God for His goodness. One more day to be thankful. One day at a time, I am counting my blessings. I am so blessed. The Lord said that when I go through the fire I shall not be burned. Thank you, Jesus. God is a way maker. I am blessed with life. It is well with my soul because I have the Lord with me.

I began to sing a variety of spiritual songs: He makes a way in the wilderness. He is God, He is holy and righteous. There is life for a look at the crucified Christ. 'Great is thy faithfulness, oh God my Father, there is no shadow of turning with Thee. Thou changest not, Thy compassion they fail not, as Thou hast been Thou forever will be. All that I needed Thine hand has provided.'

God provided pastor and TBN to pray for my strength. He gave me the word for today to which I listen. He provided supplements to strengthen my body. He provided herbs and teas for me. He gave me a special word to keep me today. God visits and heals me each day when I cry out to Him. I prayed for complete healing in Jesus' name. Great is Thy faithfulness, oh Lord.

Jesus said that we shall have what we say. I finally embraced this Word and decided to use the authority He gave me. My God is awesome. I speak *life* into the atmosphere. I speak *life* in the hospitals. Life in the word that is sent forth today. Life over my life and my family. Life all over the world. We shall live and not die! Life in every cell tissue organ in my body. It is well with my soul. *"Say ye to the righteous it shall be with him. For they shall eat the fruit of their doings."* (*Isaiah 3:10*). I slept well that night. I took Benadryl/DPH and I enjoyed a refreshing rest.

I woke at 2:00 AM, did my devotions and the *Word for Today*, and went back to bed at 4:00 AM without sleep aid, and slept well. I was at peace, and I had sweet sleep. During this sleep, I had a dream. I dreamt that my heart was racing and this caused me to panic. In the dream, I ran around calling my husband to take me to the hospital. I was not able to see through one eye.

I woke up healthy and well. I do not know if the racing of my heart was real but I denounced that, as well as any other attacks upon my sleep and rest in Jesus' name. I declared my mind, body and spirit delivered and set free in Jesus' name. I declared that I have the mind of Christ and I shall rest in the peace of God. It is well with my soul. It is God who gives life and it is He who keeps our hearts and sustains us. Jesus overcame the world, and greater is He that is in me than he that is in the world. I declared that the valves, ventricle and atrium in my heart are healed in Jesus' name. I declared normal beats, normal pulse and normal blood pressure. No weapons formed against me shall prosper. Lord guard my life, guard my family and guard my rest in Jesus' name. Lord, I place my life, my health and my family in your hands as no one can pluck us from your hands.

30

The Lord continued to teach and encourage me how to stand against circumstances by using the authority I have.

> *"Behold I give you the authority to trample on serpents and scorpions, and over all the power of the enemy; and nothing shall by any means hurt you."* Luke 10:19. NKJV

He gave me His joy to overcome difficult situations. I realized that joy is the assurance that God is in control of the world. It is quiet confidence that everything is going to be well. I choose to be right with God. God is for us He is not against us. Speak to whatever comes against you, in the name of Jesus.

So lift up your voice in thanksgiving. Find joy in thanksgiving. God wants to transform us into His will. Find joy in God's will. There is safety in the will of God.

I was awakened after a wonderful night of rest. I gave God thanks, I worshipped, I prayed, and then the Lord led me to St. John Chapter 17 where Jesus prayed for us His servants asking the great and mighty God Jehovah to keep us because we belong to Him. The Holy Spirit opened my eyes, reminding me that Jesus said, *"My peace I leave with you, My peace I give to you."* John 14:27. He showed me that His peace is a person—the Holy Spirit. Just as He is the Resurrection and He is the Life. Resurrection is a Person and Life is a Person –the Holy Spirit of God. I paused to invite the Person of the Holy Spirit, the Peace of God to dwell in me. The Holy Spirit gave me new joy.

New Mindset

I asked God to give me a new perspective on my situation. He gave me Psalm 46. "The Lord is my refuge and strength, a very present help in trouble. Therefore, do not fear, though the earth be removed and be carried in the midst of the sea." I believed God. I know whom I have believed and I am persuaded that He is able to keep that which I have committed unto Him against that day. God is our refuge and strength. What the enemy meant for evil God meant it for good. His favor surrounds me like a shield. I have the joy of the Lord, the settled assurance that He is in control.

God is powerful, God is able. When God speaks to the storm, the winds and the waves must obey Him. God is mighty to save. God is my strong tower. God is my refuge. God is my strength. God is my peace; God is my joy. God You are my health. I worship You because you are with me. God is able to do exceedingly abundantly above all that we might ask and think. God is Light, God is Love, God is Life.

On the night of May 24, 2020, I had another dream. I dreamt that I saw my sister-in-law. We appeared to be in Jamaica, West Indies with a group of nurses who were all dressed in white. We were traveling to a new location with a nursing director, and were all looking forward to this new assignment. The significance of being dressed in white suggested the righteousness of Christ.

On May 25, 2020, I had yet another dream. This time I dreamt that my family member in ICU was out of the hospital, looking very healthy and dressed to go to work. I blessed God for this dream. I magnified the Lord Jesus knowing that He is in complete control. He is Lord of all. We waited in great anticipation for this moment.

In the meantime, I developed an evening routine to facilitate my sleep habits. After dinner I would go for a relaxing walk, and before I go to bed, I would take a warm bath, read my bible, pray, and worship. I would limit my daytime naps, and limit the usage of lights, phones and television at nights. I practice muscle relaxation, exercise during the daytime, drinking warm calming tea or warm milk, and sleeping in a very cool room with relaxing music.

> Job 33:26 "He shall pray unto God, and He will be favourable unto him: and he shall see His face with joy: for He will render unto man his righteousness."

Declarations of the Word

I need not struggle or worry, when the time comes God will provide the answer. Jesus is the answer to all our problems. I cast my burdens upon the Lord with the confidence that He hears me. If I know that He hears me, I will petition Him according to His will (1John 5:14-15). All good things come from God the Father above and will come to me if I believe. I have the Holy Spirit abiding in me. Anything I ask believing, is done in Jesus' name.

I know that it is well. I will live in joy. I am anointed to overcome. I am armored with salvation as my helmet. I am robed in righteousness. I have faith, peace and truth in the Word.

Gratitude

I have discovered that gratitude is key to obtaining the answer. I am grateful and thankful for life. I am grateful and thankful that it is well and that I am employed. I am grateful that I work from home during the covid-19 pandemic. I am grateful that I am loved, that I have a home, family and friends. I am grateful that God has purpose in me. I am thankful that I am alive. I am thankful that I am healthy, I have peace, joy and hope. Thank you, God, for your Word, and that You are my comforter, keeper and healer.

Each night I fall asleep with soft inspirational music and the sound of recorded rainfall in the background. It sometimes is relaxing piano music, waves, or running water sounds. To God be the glory, He delivers. I will bless the Lord at all times his praise shall continually be in my mouth. Even though I might wake up at 2:00 AM, I bless the Lord for His goodness. I thank God, for in the valley He restores my soul. I thank God for His mercies in the valley. Anything that is wrong, God can make it right.

On a particular occasion, I decided to go before God prior to going to bed. I laid everything that worried me at the feet of Jesus. I cried out to God and He heard me from a dark place. I could feel His presence as He reached down His hand and lifted me up. He strengthened me. I am so blessed. I found peace in Him. I went to bed peaceful; however, I got very little sleep. I took Benadryl/DPH, which rarely works; but I slept from 10:00 PM until 6:00 AM. To God be the glory for He made a way.

God Uses Various Methods

Another lesson I learned from this experience is that I should not condemn anyone, because God's ways are not my ways, nor His thoughts, my thoughts. His ways are past finding out. Previously I had believed that God would not allow the use of sleep aids and I would have criticized anyone who used them. But, as I said earlier, His thoughts are not our thoughts, and I have come to realize that He would allow it for His glory.

If you are going through your valley and need to use your sleep aid, do not condemn yourself, it does not mean you will not get better—you will overcome. It does not mean you are not progressing or that you do not have faith. Embrace the knowledge that comes with each step, and trust God. What is important is that you do not get stuck at one level by condemning yourself. Forgive, and move on. Put shame and guilt aside, they are not of God. Thank you, Jesus!

As time went on, doubts would creep into my mind that I would have another sleepless night, but my trust remained in God. It was not the Benad-yl/DPH that caused me to sleep for eight hours, it was God. He gives us sleep and rest. He delivers!

> *Be still and know that I am God: I will be exalted among the heathen, I will be exalted in the earth. Psalm 46:10.*

God is my light and my salvation. Wait on the Lord be of good courage, He will strengthen thine heart. Wait I say on the Lord. Psalm 27:1&14.

It is sometimes very difficult to wait on God; however, it is absolutely necessary during the delivery process. Delivery requires patience!

Practical Wisdom

During my waiting process, my medical provider conducted blood studies to determine my overall health. It turned out that my vitamin D levels were very low. This was unusual for me because I had lived in the Caribbean all my life and had great exposure to sunlight (which synthesizes vitamin D). Now that I am living in a cooler climate and spending more time indoors, my vitamin D levels are lower. A study I read recently noted that Vitamin D deficiency is the perfect climate for fatigue and depression. Therefore, if you are suffering from anxiety and depression, ensure that your vitamin D blood levels are within normal range. I increased my vitamin D and vitamin B levels at my doctor's recommendations.

While pursuing and correcting my general health, one of my friends called from Canada to check on my family member's progress in the ICU. She prayed a powerful prayer for me when she realized that I was having sleepless nights. That night I was unable to fall asleep. I listened to scriptures and prayers, but still no sleep. I sang songs of thanksgiving.

As I sang of God's goodness, miracles began to happen. The first was that the clock shifted from 3:27 AM to 2:27 AM because of daylight savings time. God provided an extra hour for me to sleep.

The second miracle which occurred as I sang and praised God was the disappearance of the discomfort in my head.

The third miracle as I continued praising was the healing of the discomfort in my chest.

I still take DPH from time to time; however, it only works occasionally, because sleep and rest comes from God. Thank you, Jesus. With a determined mind I started to do online research regarding sleep, and also searched the bible for answers. I wanted rest and peace for my heart and mind.

Chapter Four

The Crushing

I experienced the faithfulness of God to His children about this time. While watching a program on YouTube, I saw the worship leader worshipping and soaking in God's presence. As I watched her, I longed for that level of intimacy with God and His intervention in my life. This caused me to realize that I had stepped away from my first love, and I longed to return into His arms. I used to spend time on Saturdays in my closet (my Bethel—my intimate place with God).

As I listened to the ministry, I soaked in the presence of the Holy Spirit from about 3:00 PM to 5:00 PM. There was a very severe pain in my head that worsened, as if I was having herniation to the base of my head. My body could not withstand the pressure of this crushing and pressing any longer. I reminded God that I am flesh. I cannot hold on anymore. I laid with my eyes closed, almost giving up. It was too much to bear and for too long. As the crushing pain to the back of my head worsened, I had a visitation.

There was a bright light that filled the heavens. It was too bright for my eyes to look at. I held my head down, afraid of the glow. I appeared to be a child of about six years old, dressed in white, sporting a low-cut afro, but I was unable to determine if I were a boy or girl. As I bowed my head in this strange place, a hand raised up my chin. I looked up timidly and in one glimpse realized it was the hand of the Jewish man from Nazareth, Jesus Christ. He held my hand, and I stood in disbelief. I skipped shyly with Him at first, and then we were pouncing around on the white shiny silvery clouds. It was Jesus, He heard my cry, He came. My eyes were fixed on Him as we skipped, I was no longer afraid.

I looked into His eyes and time stood still. It is true that in the presence of the Lord there is fullness of joy. Joy, unspeakable joy! There was no pain, no sickness; nothing in the world mattered, nothing else existed in the world except Jesus and me. When I finally found my voice, I said "Jesus! It is not healing that I need! I need You!" What a revelation!

Even though this experience seemed real, I was physically laying on the floor in my closet, asleep. I felt the touch of His hand to the back of my head. Immediately I was healed of my infirmity. The hand of God touched me! 'Oh, He touched me! And oh the joy that flood my soul. Something happened and now I know, He touched me and made me whole.' Hallelujah!

I woke up wide-eyed and alert. My mind was healed, my body was healed, my spirit was restored. The recording I had been listening to came to an end and I heard the host say it was 5:00 PM. I looked at the clock and it was 5:00 PM in real time. This was a visitation from Jesus. He rescued me. Thank you, Jesus! To God be the glory! The Lord brought me out. I could not be completely healed until I met Jesus the great Healer. Sickness is no match for my Lord.

I had supper, washed my hair and went for a walk. I returned home in so much joy. I was basking in the Holy Spirit. There were a few clouds in the sky as I walked but I was walking in the sunlight of the Son. His light was so bright today I gave a word from God to everyone I met.

I found new joy in Jesus. I now enjoy the things that fear had robbed me of. The Lord restored my soul. I am so thankful; I am forever grateful. There were many miracles around me today. That night I fell asleep unaided, and slept like a baby. My God is good.

During the next day I did more research regarding vitamin deficiency paying particular attention to those that can cause anxiety and depression. I found results showing lack of vitamin B6, vitamin D3, and vitamin B12 are contributing factors. I ensured that I have an adequate intake of these vitamins. I went to bed the second night listening to Benny Hinn singing: "Hallelujah! Hallelujah! Hallelujah! Hallelujah! Thank you, Jesus! Thank you, Jesus! Thank you, Jesus!" Thank you, Lord! It was my spirit that was praising God.

I asked the Holy Spirit for His presence and His peace. I asked Him to protect my sleep and give sweet dreams of Him in Jesus' name. To God be the glory. I slept from 9:30 PM to 4:30 AM. I had sweet sleep. I was well rested. To God be the glory. This time it was different—my mind, body, soul and spirit were healed. My sleep was sound, peaceful and restful.

I am back in my Bethel, where I met Jesus. Every time I feel restless, I go back in my mind to the experience of the visitation, and sweet, sound sleep immediately comes. I came to my Bethel at lunch time because I am expecting more miracles. God asked me to write every experience I have so that you, my readers, will receive your healing as well. God gave me Ephesians 2:8-9 *For by grace are ye saved through faith, and that not of yourself it is the gift of God*. I listened to Kathryn Kullman speak on grace. The Holy Spirit wants me to understand grace. It is unmerited favor from God. I am at peace in His presence.

The following day I slept all night in the peace of God in the Holy Spirit's presence. It was a place of peace and joy, so beautiful. I did not mind being awakened and relaxing in His presence laughing and communing with Jesus. Such a joy to finally find Him again. I took some DPH and finally fell asleep in peace.

I woke up refreshed. It was raining, my mind started to wander, thinking worrying thoughts. I slew them with the Word of God and rejoiced for the beautiful rainy day. I went to my Bethel and gave Holy Spirit thanks singing, "Thou art worthy, oh Lord to receive glory, honor and praise." I sang this song seven times. My mind is healed, I now have the mind of Christ.

My heart is healed, I now have the heart of God. My body is healed, I now have the breath of the Holy Spirit. I declared the blessings of God over my life. I declare I am healed seven times until my spirit hears and receives it. I declare that the anointing breaks every yoke over my life.

The Lesson I Have Learnt

From my experience, I learnt that my situation was a test. I learnt that God's hand is in my trials and I will overcome. It is all for the glory of God. I believe that by grace I am saved and that His grace is sufficient. I learnt that this too will pass.

I now know that God is the God of love. I did not understand His love for me. Love is patient, love forgives. Love is kind, love keeps no record of faults.

Love conquers, love is a weapon, for perfect love casts out fear. Love the Lord Jesus, love your neighbor, Love yourself. Know that God loves you, God cannot hate you. Be kind to yourself. Laugh, laugh and laugh.

> *God demonstrates His own love towards us, in that while we were still sinners Christ died for us.* 1 John 3:1

> *So great a love the father has bestowed upon us that we should be called sons of God.*

I learnt most of all, to apply the Word of God to every aspect of my life—even the simplest decisions. I declare it is well. The Word of God is my power. It is the Holy Spirit who is the reliever of stress. The Lord fights my battles. The battle is not mine; it is the Lord's.

A life without trials is a life without strength. Through it all we learn to trust in Jesus, we learn to depend upon His Word. Trials come to make us strong. The Holy Spirit, the Comforter will give us peace.

Here are some scriptures which can be used to relieve stress.

Romans 12:2; James 1:2-4; John 14:27; Romans 16:20; Proverbs 16:3; Romans 8:6; Matthew 11:23-30; Psalm 55:22; Isaiah 10:31; Psalm 16:18; Colossians 3:15; 1Peter 5:6-8; Psalm 56:3; Romans 8:38-39; Ephesians 5:15 -17.

God's miracles are limitless. I continue to sleep like a baby with the Holy Spirit's peace. To God be the glory! Every day, I wake up to a new life, new joy, new health, and abundance. I continue to write my pain, my defeats, my victories, and my healing so that you will benefit from the power of God. You too will face trials, note the strategies for overcoming that I have shared, because your trial is only a test.

> *Jeremiah 33:3 "Call to me and I will answer you and show you great and mighty things which you do not know." NKJV*

> *Jeremiah 29:11 "For I know the thoughts that I think towards you, says the Lord. Thoughts of peace and not of evil, to give you a future and a hope." NKJV*

When I am distracted from purpose, I struggle to sleep. At those times I take some Benadryl. I thank God for the rest I received. I have life today. It's a new day and it is well.

I have the support of powerful women of God who encourage and pray with me. Nurse Jay in Jamaica and my friend from Canada both took time out to support me. It was lovely, it was relaxing, I am so blessed.

God Changed My Story

At midday on this special day the phone rang. I noticed it was my family member calling from the ICU. Fear gripped me, because six weeks prior to his intubation in ICU his words to me were "I will call you." I had waited daily to get this call, giving up multiple times that it would happen. He called to say that he was off the ventilator but still not out of the woods yet. He had a tracheostomy in place and reported feeling awful, but well enough and stable.

As you can imagine, my heart was extremely grateful to God. I shouted "Hallelujah! God loves you very much."

He replied, "I know. God told me so when I was going through the storm." He was very tired and not in the frame of mind to speak for long. "I rejoice in You and praise You mighty God. You are a prayer-hearing God, and You deliver Your people."

During this time of praying and believing for him, I had asked God to send His Holy Spirit to the ICU to breathe for my family member. The Lord God heard my prayer, and showed me in a day vision, the shadow of someone lying on top of a body. The Holy Spirit breathed His breath of life into my family member's body and resurrected him from death to life. It had been a desperate fight for his life. His heart had stopped beating three times. But when I heard his voice on the other end of the phone, I knew that God is alive.

I asked the Lord to strengthened him and give him the spirit of joy to praise Him for this miracle. I prayed that every cell, tissue and organ in his body would be strengthened in Jesus' name.

That night I went to bed with joy. As I waited to fall asleep, my heart rate increased rapidly. I laid in bed waiting, but sleep evaded me. I did not mind because I was so thankful for the miracles of the day. I was so grateful that for once my needs were not important. My family member who was on a ventilator for over a month and believed to die soon is alive again. To God be the glory. I got out of bed picked up my bible and read three glorious chapters in St. Matthew: Chapters 4, 5 & 6. I was so blessed. I laid down again to sleep; it was late at night. I took Benadryl and fell into a deep sleep.

I woke up refreshed, thank you, Jesus. I praised God, singing the song, "I'm gonna sing, I'm gonna shout praise the Lord until the Lord delivers me from this test." He delivered my family member from death. He will deliver me; He will restore my sleep and rest. If there is trouble in your life, sing praises. God draws near, He hears and listens to the cry of His people.

The Lord God changed my story. My friend Sue called, and I asked her to pray for my healing from anxiety. She planned a diet for me which included iron, zinc, menopause supplements, multivitamins, B12 and fish oil. I ate a bowl of fruits, took my supplements and had a healthy breakfast after my devotions. I gradually drank 1 liter of water at room temperature. God changed my story.

The Holy Spirit's presence was with me. For almost seven weeks I struggled with insomnia. My husband decided to take me to urgent care. I prayed and asked God for His report. To God be the glory it was well. The Lord is on my side. The doctor suggested relaxation techniques and requested blood studies. She comforted me and prescribed antihistamine to help me sleep. I do not like taking pills. I particularly wanted to reject this drug because I am afraid of taking sleeping pills because of all the negative publicity associated with them, as well as possible addiction. I prefer taking a liquid syrup. My belief system was challenged, because I felt that it was sinful to take the pills. I felt guilty because to me it meant that God is not enough. I faced my fears and refused to condemn myself. I needed help, and God blessed medical science to help those who need help. I thank God for releasing me and freeing my mind from condemnation.

Through this incident, I was given the opportunity to share Jesus with the doctor. I shared about the first book I had written and published entitled, *"The Anatomy of Man and the Body of Christ"* and, as a result, the doctor purchased a copy. There was purpose in my pain and in my visit.

That day ended in victory. I wrote in my journal as I do daily, I read my bible, then got ready for bed after drinking green tea and taking melatonin. Thank You, Holy Spirit, you changed my story. The melatonin did not work, I had to take the liquid Benadryl. I slept well that night. Glory to God.

I woke up to a beautiful morning. I spoke life over my day, I declared it is well, I anointed myself with the oil of favor, armored myself as a conqueror and empowered myself with the mind of Christ. I armed myself with the Word of God.

That morning, I cooked green bananas, pumpkin, an egg, and codfish with steamed bak choi. I had a filling meal, then took my supplements. I ate fruits, peas and nuts, vegetables, fish, chicken and avoided processed foods. I felt good after eating, however, my chest still hurt occasionally, and my head felt light and abnormal. I was trusting God for a breakthrough.

I woke up to another new day of miracles. My family member was transferred from ICU to the ward. He was weaned off the ventilatory support, thank you Jesus. What a mighty God we serve. We rejoiced in the Lord. The Lord Jesus brought him back to life. This is a modern-day Lazarus story. I had read the story in the bible about Lazarus but did not believe that miracles like these still existed. God forgive my unbelief. I ate well and worked from home. The joy of the Lord is my strength.

I began to live by God's terms. I did not allow this feeling of sickness to force me into a corner. I continued my daily activities, enjoying my evening zoom bible study and spending time with my family. Then I would go to sleep with only the aid of the Holy Spirit—no natural sleep aid.

I slept and woke up about 3:35 AM. I was thankful for four and a half hours of rest. Who could it be but Jesus? He is my rest. There is none like you Jesus. Psalm 37: 23-24 *"The steps of a good man are ordered by the Lord; and he delighteth in his way. Though he fall, he shall not be utterly cast down for the Lord upholdeth him with His hand."* Glory to God! Thank you, Lord that You uphold me with the right hand of Your righteousness. I felt good throughout the next day. I took my iron supplements and felt better. I felt even better after going for a walk and trusting God for complete healing.

After that day I would wake in the morning praising God for His goodness. Thanking God, for each new day and singing a new song. Lord, because of who You are I give you glory. That day I read 2 Samuel 20:1-26. In this story I read how Sheba rose up against King David. Israel followed, however Judah remained loyal to King David. Amasa was sent to assemble the men of Judah in three days. He delayed his task, giving Sheba more advantage. Joab killed him and took control of all the men of Judah to fight Sheba.

When he got to Abel of Bethmaachah, a wise woman called out to Joab not to destroy the Lord's inheritance. Joab said he sought only Sheba who lifted his hand against King David. She went and with wisdom joined forces to have Sheba slain and his head thrown to Joab over the wall. So, the city was left unharmed, and King David's enemies were defeated and destroyed. Thank you, Jesus, for victory over our enemies. God protects His own, Glory to God, I am well. I have the Life of Christ in me. I live, but yet not I, but Christ who lives in me. He restored a right spirit within me. I have been changed, delivered, healed and set free. No more chains. Lord, thank You for the richness of your Word and your patience.

God's Word to me.

> *Ephesians 1:4 spoke to me: "I have chosen you Dell" says the Lord. I am sifting you to shake out old ways and awaken you to things that escaped you but are still within your reach. It is time to grab hold of what is rightfully yours and walk in it circumspectly, not as a fool but as wise, redeeming the time because the days are evil. Prayer is your unchallenged weapon with which to defeat and outwit the enemy.*

> *Isaiah 43:1-3 "When you go through the waters of adversity, I, God, the Father will be with you. When you go through the fires of purification, I, Jesus Christ, the Son will be with you. When you go through the winds of restoration, I, the Holy Spirit of God, will be with you. The Father is there with me in the waters. Jesus is there with me through the fire. The Holy Spirit is there with me in the storm.*

Thank you, Jesus, for Your presence in times of trouble. 3 John 1:2 "It is His wish that thou mayest prosper and be in good health as your spirit prospers."

God heals us with His peace. There is nowhere safer than Jesus. Where should I go but to my Lord? So I speak life over each day. I command healing over my body and my day. I declare it is well with my mind, body and spirit every day. Glory to God.

Chapter Five

Breakthrough

My family member called about 6:30 PM and related his story. He said that while he was on the ventilator, he knew nothing. Everything was like a dream. He said that while he was in that state of dreaming, he saw Satan, the dragon, very hideous, so he cried out to God and God saved him. He stated that he did not feel any pain while on the ventilator; however, the recovery was rough. His fever was very high, it felt as if the walls of the room were closing in on him. He had also developed bed sores. During that period only one person was allowed to come to his room at a time because of the ongoing pandemic. He realized that he must always remember that God saved him for a reason. He was raised to life like Lazarus. He is a modern-day Lazarus. He is more beautiful and peaceful in character in this new life.

I told him that while he was on the ventilator we had people all over the world praying for him; which, I believe, was the lifeline that God had shown me in the dream. I told him they are my associates and my church family all over the world. They are waiting for this testimony of how he overcame. I encouraged him to sing songs of worship any time his spirit feels down and to declare, like David the Psalmist, "restore unto me the joy of thy salvation and renew that right spirit within me."

Spiritual Breakthrough

There are several instruments that God will use to bring about a complete breakthrough for His children. As I listened to and absorbed myself in TD Jakes' sermon "*It is well*," I tapped into a new way of thinking which revived my spirit. I was eating well, and feeling well. I overcame discouragement because I surrendered them to Jesus. I went to bed reading the book of Revelation for the first time since this ordeal. I vividly remember that I was reading Revelation Chapter 8 when the ordeal first started, but had not continued since that time. I was renewed by the Word. I was refreshed and healed by the Word. I felt the peace and rest of deep sleep. I slept until morning.

I woke up tired, but I soaked in God's presence. God showed me new wine, new spirit, new joy, new life, new anointing, new fire and new peace. This is the season of my breakthrough. That which He is doing shall take root, bring forth, spring forth, and come forth in Jesus' name. The Holy Spirit's presence is in me, He is always near. God has healed me in Jesus' name.

My struggle had begun at the onset of the illness of my family member, but God had warned me through a dream and through His Word that He would be with me through it all.

When you pass through the waters, I will be with you; and through the rivers, they shall not overflow you.

As I was going through these struggles, I had a vision of Jesus, and He instructed me to write down my experiences every day, and as I wrote, I experienced healing miracles. Jesus assured me that it was only a test.

One of the greatest miracles was that my family member was completely healed. Additionally, I became the highest achiever at work, I recorded and sent to listeners the *"Word for Today"* daily devotional, I became a published author, and I taught from my new book on YouTube—all while experiencing my own struggles. This ordeal has increased my strength and endurance. I live every day with expectancy and anticipation. I do not take sick days, I push through, I fight through and overcome each day. God rewards me and reminds me that it is a test, so I continue to write in my **journal**. Every time sleep evaded me, I would reflect on the experience and vision of Jesus, and deep sleep would come. The Lord showed me that complete healing will come but not now, so I must write.

A life-changing moment came as I was listening one day to TD Jakes' sermon. He stated that if things refused to change in your life, then a 21-day fast would remove those stubborn things. This is a strategy for complete deliverance. I was willing to take on the challenge, the Holy Spirit confirming that this would bring my complete breakthrough. I decided and purposed in my heart that I would pray three times a day—morning, noon and night, and read the book of Job. I would read all 42 chapters, two chapters per day for 21 days. God was teaching me, and I was writing the lessons as He instructed. It is a test.

I worshipped God and thanked Him for rest. In You Lord the weary is at rest. *'Thou art worthy Oh Lord to receive Glory honor and praise.'* Lord Jesus, I dedicate these 21 days to You as I fight this battle against self, fear and disappointment. Give me victory over self for these 21 days. Let healing and deliverance come to me for the rest of my life. Thank You for the victories; give me strength to overcome the obstacles and grow in wisdom, knowledge and understanding of You Jesus. I love You, Lord because you care for me.

Now It's Your Season

Today is the day of *your* miracles! Your water has broken. There must be a state of brokenness for you to be delivered. *"A broken and a contrite spirit He cannot despise."*

There are strategies and steps to the delivery process. In the natural arena the water must break to free the baby to be delivered. The labor process requires energy and endurance.

> ➤ Lie down and open up to God
> ➤ Be naked and vulnerable before God
> ➤ Set yourself in the delivery position
> ➤ Open your mouth and declare the power of God to your fears

Push through the pain and contractions. Cry out to God. He will deliver. The Lord Jesus is molding you to be like Him. God will deliver what you labored for. Restitution or restoration will come in Jesus' name. God is faithful. Today the water is troubled—step in for your healing! Today Jesus of Nazareth is passing—be ready for your deliverance.

Let Psalm 23 be your guide today—

> *The Lord leadeth us, He goes before us*
> *He restores us to our former glory*
> *He comforts us and gives us peace.*

He anoints our heads with oil. We are empowered by the Holy Spirit as a conqueror and as an overcomer.

There are people praying for you, and waiting for the miracles. Record your miracles each day and be grateful for them.

I encourage you, reader, every day you wake up, sing, count your blessings and declare everything will be alright. My mind is stronger than my body. You must take authority over your body to make it obey the Word of God. I encourage you also to be a part of a prayer group that is always ready; a group that will wake up and pray for anyone who is in need of prayer. When you are weak, you can reach out and depend on your group to lift you up in prayer. You can draw strength from those who love you. Gather people who will not drop you but who will pray with you all the way through to deliverance. Get rid of guilt and shame, curse it from the root. Confess your faults and get help praying about it if you need to. Speak only the Word of God, which is the power of God. The power is in your mouth. Remember, you just have to *touch the hem of His garment* to be delivered from a spirit of infirmity.

Chapter Six

Engagement: Becoming Laser-Focused

Engagement

Ephesians 4:13-15 speaks to new Christians, expecting us to grow up, to increase in the knowledge of God until we become like Christ. This growth and development does not occur overnight, it is a process.

In this chapter you shall read of this process, using the book of Job.

My 21-day push towards the light started on *Day* 1 in the story of Job.

Job was Perfect.

> *Job 1:10 "Hast not thou made a hedge about him, and about his house, and about all that he hath on every side? Thou hast blessed the work of his hands, and his substance is increased in the land."*

Job realized that life begins in the womb in a state of nakedness and dependence. Job also recognized that to be delivered one must anticipate the move of God. We note that even in distress Job gave glory to God. Even in difficulties he worshipped God and even in discouragement, his praises came from a platform of victory.

One must be vulnerable, naked, open, and in a state of expectancy to be delivered.

Engagement in a natural birth is the stage of readiness, when the head or presenting part of the baby is fixed in the pelvic girdle. Contained in the head is the mind, and therefore, to be delivered from spiritual oppression, a person's mind must be focused on God. Your eyes must be fixed on Jesus. Your ears must be listening to His voice. Your mind must be prepared, determined and set on God. You must be locked in, committed, ready and in a state of expectancy. During childbirth, when the head is fixed, it is locked in, with little space to turn. It is set for the downward journey to a new life. Notice that in normal delivery it is the head that is delivered first. So, the head or mind is fixed—waiting on Jesus, waiting to begin this journey of deliverance. When the mind is delivered, the body will follow.

In Job's case he sat with his friends for seven days, speechlessly waiting on the strength and the push from God to move to the next stage of the journey. Even though his body was in pain, his mind was in greater pain grieving the great loss he suffered without any comprehension.

The state of readiness includes being prepared to push your way through. This is the position for victory. Even though Job was distressed, His eyes were on God. He knew God to be his only source of help and strength in these trials. Job summarized it in this scripture below.

Job 1:21 "Naked came I out of my mother's womb, and naked shall I return thither: The Lord gave and the Lord hath taken away; blessed be the name of the Lord."

Job was upright, full of integrity and he feared God. He was blessed with plenty. He had children and possessions in abundance. He sacrificed to God. He rose early in the morning and offered burnt offerings to God even on behalf of his children. He said, *"It may be that my sons have sinned and cursed God in their hearts."* He did this continually. However, he went through a season of drought from which he needed to be delivered.

God was so sure of Job's dedication to Him, that He even granted permission to Satan to touch Job's body but not to kill him. Throughout Job's suffering, he remained faithful to God. When things became unbearable, he would curse the day of his birth; but never God. Instead, he was careful to bless God.

> *Job 3:10-11 "Because it shut not up the doors of my mother's womb, nor hid sorrow from mine eyes. Why died I not from the womb? Why did I not give up the ghost when I came out of the belly?"*

In our Christian walk, it is essential to have supporters who can encourage us in our hour of greatest need. Eliphaz the Temanite recognized Job's contributions to the lives of others, and said to him in Job 4:3-5,

> *"Behold thou hast instructed many, and thou hast strengthen the weak hands. Thy words have upholden him that was falling, and thou hast strengthened the feeble knees. But now it is come upon thee, and thou faintest."*

He was disturbed on account of Job's suffering, thinking, most likely, that Job had sinned and God was punishing him.

The thing Job greatly feared was that his children might curse God, or that he might lose them, and what he feared is exactly what happened. In my Christian walk, I too have encouraged many like Job did, but now I was tested, now the thing I feared most came to pass, and I fainted. Now that it came to pass, I struggled.

God's purpose was fulfilled in Job's pain. The pain, the pressure and the pressing, is not to be considered as punishment, it is to prepare you for greater. The struggle, the stretching and the stress is not to kill you, it is for you to develop spiritual strength. The crushing, crisis and contractions are not to destroy you, it is for you to become a conqueror. The molding, the mess and the misery is not to distress you, it is for you to claim new miracles and ministry.

With the light of morning might come new challenges. One of my mornings was filled with chest discomfort. However, as I walked in miracles and worshipped, God gave me victory.

It is easy to become impatient because of the length of time it sometimes takes to recover from illnesses. I understand this, because for me, it had been nine weeks of trauma and seven weeks of insomnia. Now I prevailed. God has brought me out. I wrote my testimony and posted it on the web. I was healed, I felt the healing peace of God upon me after I wrote my testimony.

Psalm 102:13 "thou Oh Lord shall arise and have mercy upon Zion (Dell) for the time to favor her, yea, the set time is come."

God spoke to me through His Word that my testimony shall be written so that generations to come shall praise the Lord, and this encouraged me. God continues to take me from victory to victory, blessing to blessing and glory to glory. He will regard the prayer of the destitute and not despise their prayer.

Crushing is necessary to make new wine. It is a vital part of your life to take you to the next stage of your journey. God is doing a new thing. I used to view sleep as effortless, and took it for granted. Now I thank God for every minute of sleep He allows me to have. It is a miracle; it is priceless and it is full of joy. I enjoyed time with my husband and I give thanks for each new day, health, strength and wealth in Him. God is a good God. Oh, taste and see that the Lord is good. He watches over His word, and He watches over His saints.

Job 5:8–9 "I would seek unto God and unto God would I commit my cause. Which doeth great things and unsearchable; marvelous things without number."

10-11 "Who giveth rain upon the earth and sendeth waters upon the fields. To set up on high those that be low that those which mourn may be exalted to safety."

18-19 "For He maketh sore, and bindeth up. He woundeth and His hands make whole. He shall deliver thee in six troubles: yea, in seven there shall no evil touch thee."

Over in the New Testament we read about Nicodemus. The scriptures say that he came to Jesus by night. Even though he ran the risk of being criticized by his fellow religious leaders, he recognized that there was a lack in his life and he needed to fix the situation. So he made up his mind that he would see Jesus. He was determined to pursue his answer even if it meant coming at night. Such was the measure of his *engagement*. Jesus referred him back to the womb. *"Verily I say unto you, you must be born again."* This solution puzzled Nicodemus, and Jesus went on to explain what He meant.

It is the same today. We **must** be born of water and of the Spirit.

Chapter Seven

Descent

I continued on with the 21-day fast and prayer and am now at Days 4–6.

A very important aspect of the delivery process is the downward turn and plunge. The muscles of the uterus contract to push the fetus downwards. This is known as the *descent*. The contraction pains are undeniably severe and continue throughout the process, but it is necessary because the pressure pushes the fetus downward towards delivery. The pain, pressing and pressure cause the breaking of water.

In your life, the pushing, pain, pressure and pressing in this crushing stage may drive you to tears. Cry if you must during the crisis, cry to Jesus. He will help you to bear your cross. You cannot escape the pain during the labor and delivery process. Sometimes you may feel like it is too much. Cry out to God but do not give up. You might feel like you are going down. Yes, you must go down as you navigate the birth canal. You must travel this path to be delivered. This stage is where you are down on your face and the tears are flowing.

The Holy Spirit interprets your tears to God and brings healing. You will be delivered from that which have you bound. This is *your* birthing season. It is your ninth month. You must be broken to be blessed. You will progress from a place of restriction to a place of freedom.

As you are moving through your season of brokenness, have faith that you will get to your season of bounty and abundance. Your burdens will become blessings if you faint not.

Job was Precious to God

> *Job 8:7 "Though thy beginning was small, yet thy latter end should greatly increase."*

God promised to see us through to the season of increase. Stay focused on Jesus.

> *Job 8:20-22 "Behold God will not cast away a perfect man, neither will He help the evildoers. Till He fill thy mouth with laughing, and thy lips with rejoicing. They that hate thee shall be clothed with shame; and the dwelling place of the wicked shall come to nought."*

As you push and fight your way through, God promised to fill your mouth with laughter and your lips with joy. God's grace is sufficient to keep you through this test. *Deuteronomy 33:25 "As thy days, so shall thy strength be."*

During Day 4 of my fast, I prayed with my husband, Linton. On that day another miracle happened. I received a call regarding a new job that had been advertised. God will give us strength to face every difficulty. He will not give us more than we can bear.

On Day 5, I read Job Chapters 9 and 10.

> *God is wise in heart and mighty in strength, who hath hardened himself against him and hath prospered?*

Job 9:5-8 &10 "Which removeth the mountains and they know not: which overturneth them in His anger, which shaketh the earth out of her place and the pillars thereof tremble. Which commandeth the sun and it riseth not and sealeth up the stars. Which alone spreadeth out the heavens and treadeth upon the waves of the sea. Which doeth great things past finding out; yea and wonders without numbers."

What a mighty God we serve! With one miraculous move He shakes the earth and the world trembles.

Job 10:7 "Thou knowest that I am not wicked, and there is none that can deliver out of thine hand. (8) Thine hands have made me and fashioned me together round about; yet thou dost destroy me. (9) Remember I beseech thee, that thou hast made me as the clay; and wilt thou bring me into dust again? (10) Hast thou not poured me out as milk, and curdled me like cheese? (12) Thou hast granted me life and favour; and thy visitation hath preserved my spirit"

God is molding us into His likeness. The painful overlapping of the skull bones is part of the process. Be patient—He is working it out for your good. God showed me that now is the time of His favor.

On Day 6, I read Job Chapters 11 and 12.

Like Job, I thank God that I have overcome my struggles today. I plead the blood of Jesus over my health, my deliverance and over my family members' health in Jesus' name.

Job 11:7 "Canst thou by searching find out God? Canst thou find out the Almighty unto perfection? (16) Because thou shalt forget thy misery, and remember it as waters that pass away. (17) and thine age shall be clearer than the noonday; thou shalt shine forth, thou shalt be as the morning. (18) and thou shalt be secure, because there is hope; yea, thou shalt dig about thee, and thou shalt take thy rest in safety. (19) also thou shalt lie down, and none shall make thee afraid; yea, many shall make suit unto thee." Glory to God. God promise me that I will sleep in peace and not be a slave to fear. I will not be afraid.

Job 12:10 "In whose hand is the soul of every living thing, and the breath of all mankind. (13) With Him is wisdom and strength, He hath counsel and understanding. (14) Behold He breaketh down and it cannot be built again, he shutteth up a man and there can be no opening. (15) Behold He withholdeth the waters, and they dry up: also He sendeth them out and they overturn the earth. (16) With Him is strength and wisdom: the deceived and the deceiver are His. (17) He leadeth counsellors away spoiled and maketh judges fools. (18) He looseth the band of kings and girdeth their loins with a girdle. (19) He leadeth princes away spoiled and overthroweth the mighty.

My healing continued and I went to work healed. All is well. I applied for a supervisory position and gained favor with my supervisor and the Human Resources staff. God's favor is on me.

Chapter Eight

Flexion

*F*lexion describes the movement as the head bends and descends. As stretching and thinning occurs, it facilitates movement through the birth canal. At this point, attitude becomes very important. You must be ready, with a resolve to push. There is going to be strong resistance as labor progresses, you must bend and condition your mind to win. Position yourself to overcome.

Scripture says that we overcome by the blood of the Lamb and the word of our testimony. The right attitude means to **P**ray **U**ntil **S**oul **H**eals.

The ***molding of the head*** in delivery is a direct application of painful pressure to the head. You may feel like you are about to lose your mind. It is in the molding process that the skull bones skillfully overlap to allow the head to successfully navigate the birth canal. There is stretching and thinning. You cannot relax or sleep during delivery. To be successful, you must be alert, determined and not despair. You must remain strong in the Lord and in the power of His might.

Job's Position

Job was in pain, but he was determined to be a conqueror; and that's flexion. Determination to succeed is the attitude of a conqueror. *"Nay in all these things we are more than conqueror through Him that loved us."*

> Job 13:15 *"Though He slay me, yet will I trust in Him, but I will maintain mine own ways before Him.*

(16) He also shall be my salvation: for a hypocrite shall not come before Him. (20) Only do not two things unto me, ...withdraw thine hand far from me, and let not thy dread make me afraid.

Job 14:1 "Man that is born of a woman is of few days and full of trouble."

Days 7 to 9 for me brought peace. I spoke peace. I fought with the Word of God as my sword.

On Day 8, I prayed a powerful prayer until 10pm. I was so excited that I lost my desire for sleep; however, it was worth it; my spirit was peaceful and joyful. I was very thankful to God. He healed every cell, tissue and organ in my body. I took Benadryl and fell asleep, and woke up well as God promised. The Lord God showed me that I had sacrificed my sleep to pray for the lost, and even though I knew it was a sacrifice, I did it anyway. The Lord showed me that He delights in me.

I will praise you Lord with my every breath. The following day as I listened to TD Jakes' sermon, he reminded me that we need to bless whatever we have, even if it is not enough; just as Jesus blessed and fed 5000 persons with five loaves and two fish. It is in the blessing that little becomes much. He reminded me that we have to be broken to be blessed.

My admonition to you is that if you are not able to sleep, it is because it is time for you to be awake. You are going through the contraction pains of labor. You cannot sleep when there is a baby to be delivered. Arise and pray, seek God then go back to bed with gratitude in your heart. Guard your sleep by praying and casting all your cares on God. It is good to write what is disturbing your sleep and write a scripture of deliverance for it. List seven things for which you are grateful, then go to bed with a scripture on your mind and a song in your heart to slay the negative thoughts.

God delivered me. He delivered my head and my body through the difficult birth canal. He healed my mind, body and spirit. I can now rest after the labor process. It was a difficult birth.

> *Job 17:5 "He that speaketh flattery to his friends even the eyes of his children shall fail (7) Mine eye also is dim by reason of sorrow and all my members are as a shadow. (9) The righteous also shall hold on his way and he that hath clean hands shall be stronger and stronger".*

> *Job 18:4 "He teareth himself in his anger (5) yea the light of the wicked shall be put out, and the spark of his fire shall not shine. (17) His remembrance shall perish from the earth and he shall have no name in the street."*

On Day 9 of my fast, my family member called to say that he would be discharged the next week. Thank you, Jesus. I prayed and glorified God. That evening Sis Lena, Sis Elise and Bro Reynolds called, and they prayed with me individually rejoicing for the mercies of God.

Chapter Nine

Internal Rotation

Perseverance

As labor progresses, internal rotation begins. The head rotates into a downward position to be ready for delivery. Crowning takes place shortly thereafter, and the head is delivered.

Internal rotation speaks of the change which must begin on the inside of an individual. Change is painful, usually caused by inward conviction; but it is a sign of progress, so one must persevere through the pain. Feelings of despair may come over you, but do not give up. The darkest part of the night is just before dawn. Light is coming! Persevere and push toward the light. God will give you the inner strength to overcome the resistance. During this stage of rotation, the necessary change will be accomplished even though the body is in the same position. This is the last step before the head is completely delivered.

From a spiritual perspective, this means that a person's mind has to be delivered first. There must be a change in mentality. A paradigm shift, if you will. Mental conversion leads the way for delivery in other areas of life, including the condition of the body. The pressure experienced during this change, pushes the mind into complete deliverance.

Persevere through your struggles, your mind will be delivered. Stay committed, stay strong, you will come through. The battle may be tough, and the storm may be raging; however, Jesus is in the boat with you. He will deliver you and calm the storm. Pray for peace during this time and ask God for strength to get you through this season. He will never leave you nor forsake you. When you get to the place where you feel you cannot make it, push through to the light. Jesus will lift you up, He will give you strength and He will carry you through.

I am confident that God will see me through. He who has begun this good work will bring it to completion.

Job had friends who were present at his side and counseled him. They allowed him to talk about his problems while they listened.

> *Job 19:25 For I know that my Redeemer liveth and that He shall stand at the latter day upon the earth."*

During my season of personal spiritual delivery, I discovered a routine that very often works for me, and I would love to share that with you.

I learned to guard my sleep. I take a walk in the afternoon. I go to bed at a set time daily. I engage in a relaxing conversation with boundaries for sleep time. I make sure to have evening prayers, a warm shower, warm calming tea, calming and relaxing music; and I keep my bedroom cold.

After implementing this evening routine, I go to bed. If I wake up during the night, I pray and thank God for the first watch then ask Him for rest for the second watch.

On Day 11 of my fast I again struggled to sleep after midnight, but this time I had physical pain in my body. I got up and took a pill for the pain. The Lord gave me a calming song from Ms. True that reassured me that this too will pass. The song was *"It is alright, everything will be alright, Love is coming, Love is on the way, Love is coming."* The Lord God is Love. Love is a person and He always shows up. That which I labored for shall be restored.

> *Job 22: 28-30 "Thou shalt also decree a thing and it shall be established unto thee; and the light shall shine upon thy ways. When men are cast down then thou shalt say, there is lifting up; and He shall save the humble person. He shall deliver the island of the innocent: And it is delivered by the pureness of thine hands.*

My family and I met on Zoom for prayer for the first time since the pandemic and since my family member became ill. What a mighty God we serve! He brought all our family together because of my family member's illness and we prayed together giving glory to God. His love is all around.

Day 12 brought eight hours of glorious sleep with the help and in the presence of God by the power of His Holy Spirit. I asked God for sleep and He rewarded me. *"Thou shalt decree a thing and it shall be established."*

> *1 John 5:5 Who is he who overcometh the world, but he who believeth that Jesus is the Son of God.*

I believe you Jesus, I trust you. Thou art worthy oh Lord.

> *Job 23:10-12 But He knoweth the way that I take when He hath tried me I shall come forth as gold. My foot hath held His steps, His way have I kept, and not declined, neither have I gone back from the*

commandment of His lips. I have esteemed the
words of His mouth more than my necessary food.

Hallelujah, Glory to God!

Chapter Ten

Extension

Part of the labor process is a step called the extension. Extension happens when the increased resistance and downward force help to push the neck and head outward. After this, crowning takes place. Crowning is the actual visibility of the head before its complete delivery. After crowning, further contractions push the head outwards and there is complete delivery of the head. The head is now set free and has successfully navigated through to the light. Freedom of the head is a major step in the completion of the delivery process. This step makes way for the next stage, which is the delivery of the body.

In similar fashion, the presence of God delivers a person's mind completely and the crown of life is received as a reward. The battle of the mind is different and more difficult than the battle of the body. The mind is a strategic battle ground, and we must win this war with the strength of Jesus. In His name, we will gain victory over anything that has bound our mind. The body, on the other hand, needs deliverance from sicknesses and diseases. When our mind has been transformed to the mind of Christ, it takes priority over the physical body, and when that is done, the body is then delivered from sickness and disease.

On Day 13 sleep came and went several times during the night. At midnight I took Benadryl and fell into a brief, deep sleep. The next day I engaged in my daily soaking in the Holy Spirit. As I sat in His presence, I felt Him calling me to a deeper intimacy. I shifted my attention from me and placed it completely on Jesus, the Light of God.

He reached down His hand to lift me up off my knees; I was like a child. I was dressed in white, and Jesus playfully lifted me off my knees and we skipped on the lights in the clouds. It was a peaceful place. I need more and more and still more. In this place nothing else is important, nothing else matters. It was a place of miracles, it was a place of peace, it was the place of healing. I was touched by the Lord Jesus. I received complete healing.

I also received a call that my family member who had been discharged to the rehab facility, was discharged home. I cried, "glory to the Lamb of God." I prayed today with Pastor John giving thanks for this day of miracles.

The battle is won. Jesus came for me and healed me and the Holy Spirit went into the hospital and breathed into my family member's nostrils the breath of life. When my family member had been on the ventilator, his heart had stopped three times. I asked the Holy Spirit to go to him and breathe for him. During prayer I saw the shadow of a body lying on top of a body and this convinced me that He heard me. My family member is home now, delivered and healed. I am at home now, delivered from pain and insomnia. Thank you, Jesus!

On Day 14, I read Job Chapters 27 and 28.

My experiences in the presence of Jesus, the Light of the world has always been very peaceful. The next night I again slept in peace. It was a deeper sleep than any sleep I had before, glory to God. I worshipped God because my family member was finally at home in his own bed. I too was enjoying deep, restful sleep.

As I slept that night, I dreamt about a nurse who worked in the USA. God indicated to me that nursing was indeed her calling. When I reached out to her, she was crying because she had been accused and scorned. I prayed with her and encouraged her and sent her in the strength of the Lord.

> *Job 27:3 All the while my breath is in me, and the Spirit of God is in my nostrils.*

> *Job 28:28 Behold the fear of the Lord that is wisdom and to depart from evil is understanding.*

To God be the glory!

I continue to enjoy praise and worship music on my way to sleep, and on Day 15, I slept very well. I listened to the song by Heidi entitled: "light". I kept my eyes on Jesus and the experience I had of Him surrounded by Light.

I understood from my experience that in order to maintain the healing He has provided, we must remain in His presence. God is a good God. He gives His beloved sleep. His Word encourages us to *"set our affections on things above not on things in this world."* Sleep is from above. All we need is Jesus.

There were several other blessings that followed my deliverance: I was given a key to my church; I was given the opportunity to lead intercessory prayer with three persons in attendance, and I received prophetic dreams from God. I also was given a glimpse of heaven and as a result, I will never again lose sight of Jesus. I was

consumed by the Holy Spirit and shaken off my feet; I
laughed in the spirit.

.

Chapter Eleven

Restitution

During my study of the book of Job, I note the need to wait for restitution. After the head is delivered, we must patiently wait for restitution. Restitution is a part of total delivery, and total delivery requires patience.

Restitution is the movement of the head turning in the opposite direction of where it had already turned. This movement permits the head and neck to realign with the body for a safe delivery of the body. After the head leaves the birth canal, the body must be delivered quickly, if not the fetus will die. Restitution is a vital part of the overall process. Even though the contraction pain is almost unbearable, you must push to get to the final stage. There is extensive stretching and bearing down to deliver the body.

The head successfully navigates the birth canal and is delivered. Even though the head is free, the body is still confined in the birth canal and must be delivered speedily, or complications may arise. The head which is already delivered now changes and turns to align again with the body for the delivery of the baby.

It is at this point that support is necessary. A good support system will encourage you to maintain good breathing and to continue to push through. God has brought you to this place and His presence will see you through to complete victory. He provides supportive sisters and family members to give you encouragement.

At this juncture in my study of the book of Job, I incorporated a family outing during the day. My family and I went fishing. Fishing is a wonderful way to exhibit patience. So on Day 16 I had a wonderful and exciting trip. As a result of the outing that day, I was late for my midday time with God; however, I read the Word in Job, prayed, and rested in the presence of God.

Patience

During this covenant with God for the 21 days, I read two chapters from the book of Job daily, met with God and prayed three times daily.

It was during this season that I got a visitation from Jesus and the healing from the Holy Spirit. In the presence of the Lord there is fullness of joy. As the deer pants for the water, so my soul longs after thee.

On one occasion during this 21-day fast, I dreamt that I was at my house in Jamaica with my husband. I did not see the tenant who occupied the house, but I noticed that the yard was overgrown with weeds. I also noticed that the new gate was missing and the old one was in its place. I noticed an expansion happening in the house across the street from my house. The roof of the large house next door was off and the house was abandoned. The house next to this home had a huge wall built up. The street looked strange; however, my house had no noticeable change except for the weeds and the old gate. From these observations, I surmised that the residents of these homes were going through spiritual warfare. "Lord, I prayed, heal the families that live on this street."

On Day 17 I again went fishing with my husband. At the end of the day, I was too tired from the trip to fall asleep immediately. I employed the strategy given by the Holy Spirit and focused on Jesus. I entered into His presence and fell asleep and slept all night.

> *There remains therefore a rest for the people of God. For he who has entered His rest has himself also ceased from his works as God did from His. Hebrews 4:9-10 NKJV*

Thank you, Jesus, help me to rest in you. I will meditate on Your word.

> *Job 33:4 The Spirit of God has made me and the breath of the Almighty gives me life.* Verse 15 says, *"in a dream in a vision of the night, when deep sleep falls upon men, while slumbering on their beds, (16) Then He opens the ears of men, and seals their instruction." Verse 26: "He shall pray to God, and He will delight in him, He shall see His face with joy; For He restores to man His righteousness." NKJV*

I continue to relive my experience of the presence of Jesus, and the light of heaven that healed and saved me on Day 18. Jesus is greater than time. He exists outside of time. In His presence, nothing else has power; only Jesus exists. He is light. I meditate on His words. I soak in His presence. I pray, read the word and worship.

I have slept very well since I experienced Jesus. Thank you, Lord. Even though I might go to bed late, I sleep well.

> *Job 36:11 If they obey and serve Him, they shall spend their days in prosperity and their years in pleasure (15) He delivers the poor in their affliction*

and opens their ears in oppression. (26) Behold, God is great and we do not know him, nor can the number of his years be discovered. NKJV

In the midst of victory, the enemy tried to steal my joy. It happened that I had an altercation with a nurse colleague that did not resolve amicably. I was angry. When our family met for prayer that day, my family member led us in prayer. I thank God he is well enough to pray with the family. After that, I again went fishing with my husband and went to bed late. That night my mind went over the details of the altercation with the nurse. I asked God to help me to forgive her so I could sleep. I took Benadryl and went to sleep.

Chapter Twelve

Expulsion

Prevailing

*E*xpulsion marks the delivery of the entire body. This means that the head and body are completely free. The placenta is delivered next. The expulsion stage is the beginning of new life, new light and new love.

I woke up on Day 19 with joy. I have joy, as long as I have Jesus, I prayed for God to help my colleague and me to forgive each other. I made peace with God, and let it go. In the expulsion stage, it is necessary to relieve oneself of all harmful feelings.

> *Job 38:12-13 Hast thou commanded the morning since thy days, and caused the dayspring to know his place, that it might take hold of the ends of the earth, that the wicked might be shaken out of it?*

Command your morning, says the Lord! Prophesy to your spirit. Decree a thing and it shall be established. I declare and decree that "in all these things I am more than a conqueror through Him that loved me."

I watched a sermon entitled, 'Let it go" and asked God to show me how to love, forgive and have mercy. We must show love and compassion to forgive. The answer to reconciliation is love. "Love your family member as yourself."

Whom the Lord loves, He chastens.

On Day 20 of my covenant, I continued with my daily declarations, as they are the key to a victorious day. I declare that the battle is for the Lord's. I declare that I am a conqueror and an overcomer. I have light, love and life in Christ. I win with Jesus. I had been attacked the previous day with unforgiveness, and it threatened my sleep, but I overcame with love and slept for eight hours. Love freed me.

To be victorious in your life, you need a spirit of love, grace, mercy and compassion. You have to be able to empathize with the struggles of others. When you love, you forgive. Love lifted me. Thank you, God, for your power. You are God Almighty.

This is my 21st day!! Glory be to God. When we stand in faith, God always shows up. I cover my body with the blood of Jesus and wait upon God. When it seems as if the night is almost over and I have not slept, I reach out and touch the hem of His garment, and He always responds with sweet sleep even if it is a short sleep.

> *"They that wait upon the Lord shall renew their strength. They shall mount up with wings as eagles. They shall run and not be weary, and they shall walk and not faint." Isaiah 30:41*

Thank you Lord Jesus I have learnt how to wait. It was a painful wait, but it was worth it. I waited in obedience for 21 days. I pressed and pushed through the final night and I was delivered. Thank you, Jesus.

In Job 42:10 we read,

> *"And the Lord turned the captivity of Job when he prayed for his friends."*

The Lord also gave Job twice as much as he had before. Glory to God. I prayed for my friends, and as I did, God delivered me and gave me peace.

Love is the answer to all our problems. It was love that helped me to navigate through the darkness of my personal birth canal of illness. There is also purpose in everything we go through. I believe that the purpose served was to give birth to this book. God delivered me from anxiety and depression so that I can testify with conviction that He is able to do the same for anyone. I overcome by the blood of the Lamb and by the word of my testimony.

Potential Obstacles

The Labor process requires energy, strength, and perseverance.

In Utero there are many obstacles that can cause failure to progress. One such is when the bones of the pelvis (which are sharp) trap the head. This can prevent the head from moving forward. The experienced midwife can skillfully assess the situation and intervene so that both mother and baby are delivered safely. Spiritually, this means that a person's history may involve generational curses that can interfere with their spiritual delivery. Curses such as fears, lies and negative words declared over you and/or your family can trap the mind. A person must ask God to break these curses that keep him or her shackled or bound. Your mind must break free.

There are other obstructions such as fibroids that compete with the fetus for nutrients and space in the uterus. In the spirit realm this represents anger, pride, strife that cause you to feel bigger and mighty in the flesh. These are destructive in the spirit. Pray for deliverance against these.

Stored waste like a full bladder or full rectum can also vie for space and can narrow the space in the birth canal, obstructing delivery. Spiritually, this means that gossip, envy and covetousness in the soul can obstruct the delivery process. These are toxic and should be eliminated.

Disease in the mother's birth canal can also affect the delivery process because it can be transferred from mother to child. This is known as congenital illnesses. Spiritually, our sinful nature can affect future generations. Ezekiel 36:25 "*I will sprinkle clean water on you and you shall be clean.*" God can cleanse all sins. Pray and ask God for healing.

There are also complications when the shoulders are too wide to be delivered. This requires skills of the midwife. In previous years, they would break the shoulder bone to save the life and deliver the baby. Spiritually, this difficulty means you have to persevere and experience brokenness to get to the next level. It means you will need skillful mentors who can discern and help you navigate in this season.

There must be a breaking in order to be free and to be delivered. As is the case in life, the delivery process comes with obstacles. There are difficulties that you must overcome. *Come unto me all ye that labor and are heavy laden and I will give you rest*. Push through the pain in the struggles. God has deposited in you the strength you need to overcome. Deut. 33:25 *As thy days so shall thy strength be*. The pain is the evidence that God is bringing you through a test. The victory over each obstacle will give you power to overcome those ahead.

As you navigate the birth canal, God has provided skillful mentors and midwives to help guide the process. Pray and ask God to send your destiny helper, your mentor or your midwife. God always makes a way; in the same way He provided Elijah to mentor Elisha.

Chapter Thirteen

Welcome to the Light

Solidifying Your Freedom

As God delivers you from a life of bondage to a life of freedom, you might need to take a further step to solidify your freedom. It involves the healing process, and often requires counseling or therapy. We cannot overlook this very important step.

When you are opened to receiving counseling, you acknowledge that you are experiencing an emotional weakness and you need assistance to find healing. People sometimes skip this step because of the stigma associated with mental health. This stigma causes many persons to refuse this therapy with the result that they fall into relapse. In natural childbirth, without a form of intervention, it is very easy to fall into postnatal depression after delivery. One must rest from hard labor. If a person becomes a victim of postnatal depression, it can cause them to destroy their offspring—that for which they have lovingly labored.

In similar fashion, it is of utmost importance that a new Christian is counseled in the Word of God in order to grow in wisdom and become a true disciple. A disciple's growth is dependent on his time spent being taught the Word and applying the knowledge of the Word to his life. Having someone to listen and help bear his or her burden contributes to the strength of the Believer. Sitting and talking with a trusted therapist about your fears helps to alleviate the weight you carry. This is crucial as we were created to exist in community. Intervention such as teaching, mentoring and guidance is necessary for optimal mental health as well as spiritual prosperity. Just as physical rest is necessary after a natural childbirth, resting in the Holy Spirit is crucial to one's spiritual progress.

The counseling stage was difficult for me because I did not see the importance of a therapist. However, God showed me that just as I spent time with my bible-study teacher being taught in the Word, I needed a therapist to give sound mental health guidance during my journey.

I obeyed God and found it was impactful talking to someone who can give valuable mental health guidance for healing. It was refreshing and relaxing, receiving nonjudgmental guidance and finding peace in this process.

Welcome to Freedom

Stand still, says the Lord, and see the salvation of your God. The battle is not yours it is the Lord's. Whatever circumstances present themselves, stand still and prevail. You shall not die but live and declare the works of the Lord. You are a conqueror, you are an overcomer and you are a victor. You, also have prevailed. You have made it from a life of confinement to a life of freedom. Like the natural baby, you have made it from a life of darkness to the light. You have made it from a life of total dependency to a life of independence!

You prevailed and you are now in the light of God. You prevailed, and you are now breathing the Breath of

Life—the Holy Spirit. You prevailed, and you experienced the love of Jesus.

You are delivered, you are born, you are set free! The battle is over. You have successfully navigated the spiritual birth canal. You are perfect in the sight of God. You are a precious Child of God.

Continue to persevere in God. Continue to be patient in God. You have prevailed because you have conquered the difficulty of the birth canal, and arrived at the light.

Continue to push through the light to your next experience in Jesus. Just like the woman with the issue of blood, she pressed through to her healing. You must keep your eyes focused on Jesus. You must see life through the eyes of Jesus by spending time in His presence and in His Word. It was His love that helped me to forgive. Perfect love casts out fear.

When we experience an encounter with Jesus and feel the manifold love that He has for us, that love heals our hearts and changes our lives. Knowing that Jesus loves us personally makes it easier to trust Him. Jesus helped me to understand that the difficulties, stress and problems we face daily are temporary. I need to look to Him for the things that are eternal. I learned to hand all my troubles over to Jesus and trust Him to fix them because I know He loves me. When you love Jesus, you believe His Word. Ask God for an eye-opening experience of Him and His love. Seek His presence and seek His face. Your labor of love will bring forth life. A life of love, a life of joy and a life of peace.

Learn to prophesy to your circumstances. Say to them, "when I go through the fire, I shall not be burned."

Recognize that it is a test for you to know the love of God for you, for you to trust Him and find strength in His power. So, speak to your mind and tell it who your God is. Remind your mind that:

Problems are no match for God. God always shows up; We have a loving relationship; God gave me His word; God taught me to live one day at a time; God taught me that this will pass; God calm storms; God gives rest; God heals mind body and spirit; God says we overcome by the blood of the Lamb and the word of our testimony; God will take us to the other side and into our season of blessings; in all things I am thankful to God.

Chapter Fourteen
The Call to Midwives

The Lord God has called midwives to help those who need to be delivered. Our job is to help them to navigate the difficult birthing process. If God has called you as a midwife, be obedient to the call because many lives will be delivered and set free. I was a registered nurse who helped to heal those who are sick and were admitted to the hospital for care. This is what the church is. It is a place where people who are sick and tired of living in sin can come and get the care they need to become physically, mentally, emotionally and spiritually healthy and strong.

During my career as a nurse, as I was working in community nursing and assigned to the clinics, I studied midwifery and became a practicing midwife, but I did not immediately recognize this as a move of God. In the Bible, midwives were asked by Pharoah to kill the Israelite boys at birth; however, the midwives wisely informed Pharoah that because the Israeli women were very active, they delivered the babies before the midwives could intervene.

When God has decreed a plan for your life, nothing can stop it. In my case, God made the way for me to be chosen to study as a midwife. My original plans did not include midwifery, because my husband was in the USA and I wanted to do the US license exam and then migrate from Jamaica to the US. However, when I enquired of God, He confirmed it as His plan for my life. I obediently took on my new assignment. The Lord wanted me to be a nurse and a midwife to help deliver and reduce complications of birth in the natural and in the spiritual. At my interview for this training, I recalled being asked why I would want to become a midwife at my age—why now? They asked. I remember responding, "Why not now?" I remember explaining that I was on a journey and my journey had brought me to this place at this time so I was willing to embrace it.

My employment journey began with a job as a bank teller and supervisor. I then worked as an airline staff member, before my nursing career. I studied at the University School of Nursing and graduated with a Bachelor's degree as a Registered Nurse. I was voted as the class representative both in nursing school and in midwife school.

Under the direction of the Holy Spirit, the prayer meetings I conducted with the midwives on Wednesdays after classes resulted in many astounding miracles. The group was strengthened because the results were measurable. It was so fruitful that lecturers and students from other groups in the Nursing School would come to these meetings for their breakthrough. I remembered God instructing me to lay my hand on each nurse and declare over each one the specific fruit of the Spirit as He advised. God showed me that as midwives, our hands are always the first to touch these sterile, innocent, precious gifts from Him. He also showed me that the midwives should declare the same gift of the Spirit they received over the babies they delivered. I received these profound instructions eagerly and with joy; but unfortunately, I forgot them when we met on the following Wednesday for prayer. I believe this happened because I was in student mode.

Prior to the meeting that Wednesday, I was confronted by a student in front of the class. The nursing student shouted at me. I was about to shout back when the lecturer looked at me in a scolding way that reminded me that I knew better. It made me angry because I felt that everyone was looking at me to do what Jesus would do. I was angry because I wanted to get back at the nurse. I was so upset that I could not pray at the prayer meeting. Everyone turned up, waiting on me to begin, but I could not. My heart was full and heavy. I turned and cried out to God to heal my heavy heart. I confessed to Him that I cannot pray to Him with this weight on my heart and I need Him to help me. God showed up.

God is faithful and patient, and He reminded me of the instructions He had given me which I had forgotten, knowing that I would seek Him after this attack. I asked Him to forgive me. I now had peace with myself, with the nurse and with God. The attack helped me get back on track, to get my focus back on God. That evening we had a wonderful worship service. I prayed with the nurses and declared the Spirit of Love, Peace, Joy, Patience, Humility, Faithfulness, Gentleness, Self-control, Goodness. As I walked over and laid my hand on each nurse, God instructed me which Fruit to declare over her. The nurses were instructed to declare these Fruits of the Spirit over each baby they deliver because we are the first persons to see and touch the babies even before the mothers who had carried them.

Each nurse was amazed! One nurse over whom I declared the spirit of joy asked me: "how do you know my alias name is Joy?" Another nurse over whom I declared the spirit of peace asked, "how do you know that I desperately need this peace today?"

As I declared God's instructions over each nurse, I observed that the nurse who shouted at me was crying—and had been crying from the beginning of the prayer meeting. She realized what she had done and was struggling with guilt. When I got over to her, the Lord said 'hug her.' I hugged her and felt the pain of the attack drained from my heart and God filled my heart with love.

Thank you, Jesus, for your peace. My mission was accomplished that evening, and I walked into victory.

Today, for those who will be delivered when reading this book, I declare the ninefold Fruit of the Spirit with a double dose of love, peace and joy. I also declare that you will transfer this God-given spirit to those to whom you will be assigned. This is important because it is necessary for you to perpetuate the goodness of God in someone else's life. I encourage you to develop relationships; start by mentoring a child. Always keep your eyes and focus on Jesus, and continue to live by the Fruit of the Spirit.

During the process of natural child birth, there is still one more step to be completed. The umbilical cord is still attached to the placenta, and needs to be cut. Similarly, even though you have been delivered from bondage, there is still a connection with your past life. The 'umbilical cord' needs to be cut. There needs to be a disconnection from your past life of darkness, restriction and dependence. You have come into the light, into a large place where you can function on your own with assistance. You are set free.

> *Stand fast therefore in the liberty by which Christ has made us free, and do not be entangled again with a yoke of bondage. Galatians 5:1 NKJV.*

God's blessings be multiplied to you.

REFERENCES

Ayangoke, Elizabeth O. (2012), *The Elizabethan Midwifery Book*

Peterson, Gail, (May 2023), *When Does a Fetus have a Heartbeat?*- Human Life International

OTHER BOOKS BY THE AUTHOR

The Anatomy of Man and the Body of Christ

Available in English and Spanish at
https://eaglespublisher.com

or by contacting the author at

dell.walters@yahoo.com

Also available online:
Amazon.com

www.ingramcontent.com/pod-product-compliance
Lightning Source LLC
LaVergne TN
LVHW021537080426
835509LV00019B/2690

```
* 9 7 9 8 9 8 7 8 5 2 2 7 9 *
```